DATE DUE

JAN 1 1 2010

Media, Politics, and Asian Americans

THE HAMPTON PRESS COMMUNICATION SERIES
Political Communication
Gianpietro Mazzolini, *series editor*

Media, Politics, and Asian Americans
H. Denis Wu and Tien-Tsung Lee

forthcoming

Antipolitics and Government: DeGaulle, Reagan, Berlusconi
Donatella Campus

Democracy in a Network Society
Kenneth L. Hacker and Jan van Dijk (eds.)

Media, Politics, and Asian Americans

by

H. Denis Wu
College of Communication
Boston University

and

Tien-Tsung Lee
William Allen White School of Journalism
and Mass Communications
University of Kansas

HAMPTON PRESS, INC.
CRESSKILL, NJ 07626

Printed in the United States of America

Library of Congress Cataloging-in-Publication Data

Wu, H. Denis.
   Media, politics, and Asian Americans / by H. Denis Wu and Tien-Tsung Lee.
       p. cm. — (The Hampton Press communication series. Political communication)
   Includes bibliographical references and index.
   ISBN 978-1-57273-870-6 (hardbound) — ISBN 978-1-57273-871-3 (pbk.)
   1. Asian Americans and mass media.   2. Asian Americans—Press coverage.
3. Asian Americans—Politics and government.   4. Communication in
politics—United States.   I. Lee, Tien-Tsung.   II. Title.

   P94.5.A75W8 2008
   302.23089'95073—dc22   2008047693

Hampton Press, Inc.
23 Broadway
Cresskill, NJ 07626

Contents

*Chapter 4 is written by H. Denis Wu and Ralph Izard

Acknowledgments

H. Denis Wu

This book could not have been finished without the help from lots of people. I owe a great deal to my capable research assistants, Jane Dailey and Suping Zhang. This book project was generously funded by a Louisiana State University (LSU) research grant and Manship School professorships. I am grateful to the LSU administrators who believe in this line of works and agreed to provide needed funding. Thanks to Ralph Izard, the project examining Asian American staff and its relationship to news quality could be implemented, and its end result adds an essential piece to this book. Three Asian American public office seekers (Gary Locke, David Wu, and Matt Fong) and other campaign professionals included in this book gave us their precious time and insights. I am also indebted to many mentors during and after my graduate programs, particularly Jane Brown, George Gerbner, Donald Shaw, and Robert Stevenson, who laid a solid foundation for my research skills and so much more. Many of my colleagues, particularly Renita Coleman, have been extremely helpful, too. My co-author, Tien, is truly a pleasure to work with—I am enormously fortunate to have him on board for this book-writing journey. These past few years, although slightly bumpy for both of us, have turned out not just fulfilling, but fruitful. I am glad that this book is finally finished. Additionally, I would like to thank my family members for their immense support, understanding, and occasional pushes. Last, I would like to dedicate this book to Naomi, the first all-American girl in the family.

Tien-Tsung Lee

My foremost gratitude goes to my co-author, Denis, who invited me to collaborate on this project a few years ago at an annual conference of the Association for Education in Journalism and Mass Communication in Washington, DC. Over lunch we wrote down the basic structure of the book. Some original ideas were kept and others have morphed into something entirely different. Looking back, it is amazing that a simple outline has turned into a real book. This has been an exciting intellectual adventure from which, and from Denis, I have learned much as a researcher and writer.

I want to thank many of my colleagues, friends and graduate assistants for their feedback, encouragement, editing and proofreading, advice on statistics and writing academic articles/books, collecting literature, and other forms of support and assistance in this long process. These wonderful individuals include Mark Havens, Curt Blumer, Paul Brandenburger, Alan DeValle, Greg Halloran, Keith Wolter, Faith Hwang, Gary Hicks, Kuang-Kuo Chang, Stephen Silha, H.W. Martin, Moon Lee, John Irby, Julie Andsager, Bruce Pinkleton, Doug Hindman, Dave Demers, Roberta Kelly, Yuki Fujioka, Bill Ryan, Barbara Barnett, Kerry Benson, Ann Brill, Alex Tan, Yvonnes Chen, Masahiro Yamamoto, Ming Wang, Lingling Zhang, Gordon Alloway, Chris Brott, McKay Stangler and Shaun Hittle. This is also a good opportunity to thank the reviewers and editors of various journals, conferences and publishing firms who have provided helpful feedback when earlier versions and portions of this manuscript were submitted for review. Last but not least, my deep appreciation goes to my parents for their never ending support, and my mentors/teachers who taught me how to do research – Wayne Wanta, Arnold Ismach, Jim Lemert, Ann Maxwell, Jerry Medler, Bill Wells, Phil Tichenor, Tsan-Kuo Chang, Ron Faber, Bill Flanigan and Ted Gerber.

Chapter 1

Introduction

ISSUES BEHIND A TRUE STORY

In April 2005, a 34-year-old Korean American named Jun Choi was running in the Democratic mayoral primary in Edison, New Jersey. The race was tough and the political debate was heated. During the campaign, a local radio (WKXW-FM) talk show host commented on Choi's candidacy, saying, "no specific minority group or foreign group should ever, ever dictate the outcome of an American election, I don't care if the Chinese population in Edison has quadrupled in the last year, Chinese should never dictate the outcome of an election. Americans should." As expected, Asian Americans and others in Edison reacted angrily to the comment and immediately demanded that the host be fired (Hinckley, 2005).

There are at least two obvious problems with the assertions made by this radio personality. First, only American citizens can run for public office in the United States. Jun Choi is an American. Second, Choi is Korean American. Like the fact that not all European Americans' ancestors came from Germany, not all Asian Americans are of Chinese descent.

The radio host's remarks may simply have been intended as mere entertainment or comedy, as he vehemently claimed (Hinckley, 2005). However, the remarks are racist and bely the host's ignorance regarding the distinction between Asians and Asian Americans, as well as the ethnic diversity within the Asian American community.

At a deeper level, the unfortunate comments imply that Asian American citizens should not be accorded the full and same rights of political participation in the United States. Yet for many Asian Americans, what this scenario exemplifies is only the tip of the iceberg. The radio host's prejudiced views likely represent the mindset of many Americans who know or care little about Asian Americans. Yet when the ignorant opine in public, it reveals the fissure between Asian Americans and others in the nation.

This incident also underscores an agonizing reality for many Asian Americans, namely, that no matter how many generations their families have been in the United States, Asian Americans are not immediately seen as fellow citizens by many of their non-Asian American counterparts. Instead, second-, third-, and even fourth-generation Asian Americans are still likely to be viewed as foreigners who speak little or no English. Asian Americans simply have not yet shed their perceived foreignness (R. Lee, 1999). The murder of Vincent Chin in 1982 is an old and extreme but still relevant example of this misperception. Chin, a Chinese American, was mistaken for being Japanese and was killed by two Detroit autoworkers who blamed competition from Japanese car makers for losing their jobs (R. Lee, 1999; Yip, 1997).

Because of this perceived foreignness, it comes as no surprise that many Americans do not immediately think of Asian Americans as potential public office holders. To many, Asian Americans just do not look like governors, congressional representatives, or mayors. The percentage of public offices held by Asian Americans—compared with members of other races—is much smaller. Not surprisingly, mass media rarely portray Asian Americans in a way that would make the general public feel that Asian Americans can win elections, hold public offices, and actually govern or make laws.

Let us put the 2005 incident mentioned earlier in an even broader context. We see a clear anti-immigrant trend in today's political climate across the country. For instance, English is declared the sole official language in various localities. Laws are passed to prevent illegal immigrants from receiving various benefits. More employers are penalized for hiring workers without proper authorizations (Feagans, 2006; Har, 2007; "Referendum Revelations," 2006; Riccardi & Gaouette, 2006; "Signs of Hope," 2006). Is the way Asian Americans are perceived and treated by their fellow Americans part of this trend or are they dealing with a different type of mentality? We want you to be the judge after reading this book.

WHY WE WROTE THIS BOOK

The intersection of media, ethnicity, and politics constitutes an important new area for Asian American studies, communication, and political science research. Politicians and political scientists have gradually realized that democracies and politics simply cannot function effectively (or efficiently) without the media. Thanks to outstanding researchers, many of whom are cited in this book, there is already a significant body of literature in Asian American studies. Building on their contributions, this book, we believe, sheds new light on a relatively neglected area of study—an interdisciplinary investigation into mass media and race politics involving Asian Americans.

Our academic background and primary research interest is mass communication. Therefore, we begin this book from a mass media perspective. We, like many other observers, believe that politics in this country is, to a large extent, influenced and shaped by how and whom the media present, highlight, or ignore.

Although Asian Americans are viable candidates in the elections in which they participate, without prominent images of successful Asian American politicians in the media, they have a harder time persuading the general public that they are as qualified as politicians who are not of Asian descent. This issue of perceived electability is particularly important to Asian Americans because they represent only about 4% of the U.S. population, and this small percentage means less voting power. Also, unlike other minorities that tend to cluster in certain geographic regions and form voting blocks, Asian Americans are more dispersed, share no single common language or religion, and, above all, possess enormously diverse political perspectives and backgrounds. (For a comprehensive review of Asian Americans' political participation, including coalitions between Asian ethnic groups in some occasions, please see Lai, 2000; Lien, Collet, Wong, & Ramakrishnan, 2001; Lien, Conway, & J. Wong, 2004). Furthermore, the moniker *Asian American* probably strikes many who bear this identity as a novel, government-assigned label. They likely prefer a more specific and appropriate label, such as Korean American or Filipino American. As a result, Asian Americans running for office almost always need to seek support from other ethnic groups, both Asian and others who may or may not hold positive attitudes toward them.

As 4.2% of the U.S. population in 2000 (U.S. Census Bureau, 2002), Asian Americans are more likely to be understood indirectly through media portrayals. Unfortunately, most research has shown that stereotypical and negative images of Asians and Asian Americans are pervasive in the media, including TV and movies (e.g., Hamamoto, 1994; R. Lee, 1999; Wong, 1978). Some Americans' discriminatory attitudes toward Asian Americans may have been influenced by high-profile, notorious incidents, including the legal case against nuclear scientist Wen Ho Lee, who was wrongfully accused of being a Chinese spy (W. Lee & Zia, 2002).

Nevertheless, the days of Charlie Chan and Dr. Fu Manchu—fictional characters who stereotypically and often negatively represented Asians and Asian Americans in popular American culture (Kim, 1982; R. Lee, 1999)—are hopefully gone for good. In a different media sector—advertising—Asian Americans have begun to be depicted as being highly educated and members of affluent circles, including playing the roles of financial professionals and computer specialists (Paek & Shah, 2003; Taylor & Stern, 1997; Taylor, Landreth, & Bang, 2005). For example, a 1999 TIAA-CREF print ad featured an Asian-looking man with a Japanese-sounding last name, Hashimoto, who had earned an A.B., M.S., M.D., J.D., and M.O.H., chose to participate in a TIAA-CREF retirement program. These more recent images of Asian Americans suggest an ethnic group understood to be a "model minority," rather than the negative and clichéd media images of the past, such as coolies, bandits, hookers, laundrymen, gooks, gangsters, and restaurant owners (Hamamoto, 1994; R. Lee, 1999). Yet there is no guarantee that the more positive, yet equally as stereotypical images will continue. In the decades following World War II, images of and attitudes toward Asian Americans have swung from negative to positive, back and forth like a pendulum across the shared history of Asia and the United States changing with Americans' sometimes ambivalent, sometimes vexed relationship with Asia (Isaacs, 1958).

The prior examples (also see Feng, 2002; Ghymn, 2000; Hamamoto & Liu, 2000) show that many scholars interested in how Asians and Asian Americans are portrayed in mass media have focused on entertainment-oriented fares such as TV commercials and dramas, fictions, and Hollywood-made films. A number of these scholars argue that, through the depiction of Asian Americans, such films can represent as well as underscore the ethos of mainstream American culture. Films also can powerfully influence popular attitudes toward ethnic groups in general. For instance, one would instantaneously think of the mafia when it comes to Italian Americans, thanks to Francis Ford Coppola's *Godfather* series and other gangster films dating back to the 1930s. Research shows Hollywood's products have corresponded well to U.S. foreign policies and public opinion toward Asian Americans. For example, Isaacs (1958) chronicled the images of Asian Americans presented in the movies and found that the images of the Chinese were portrayed positively during WWII, a period when China was an American ally, but the images took a 180-degree turn when the communist regime took over China. Another vivid example is that the cinematic representations of Japanese culture were negative during the 1980s, when the economic power of Japan reached its peak. Many films released during the period showed the Japanese as greedy, ambitious, and covertly scheming to control the United States.

Because it is still the main mode of entertainment for most American households, TV also has received much scholarly attention. For example, Wu (1996) compared the fate of Chinese and American characters and discovered that plot formulas for each of the groups were strikingly different. Most Chinese actors/actresses were given minor roles, with overwhelmingly negative images. To enjoy a happy ending in typical prime-time American TV shows, Chinese characters often had to produce much more than hard work and good deeds; indeed, they often had to be helped by White Americans to succeed. Another example in this line of research is a landmark study by Hamamoto (1994), who also documents negative treatments of Asian American characters in TV programming. Aside from these examples, many other empirical studies of TV shows unveil structurally slanted and culturally demeaning representations of Asian Americans.

Until the present study, excepting a handful of racist incidents that generated public outcry, comparatively little attention has been paid to the news media's portrayals of Asian Americans. The notorious, irresponsible reporting surrounding the alleged spying by Wen Ho Lee is a case in point. Insinuations about figure skater Michelle Kwan's alien status in the coverage of two Winter Olympic games (see chapter 5, this volume; Fancher, 2002; Lyke, 2001) did not seem to attract as much public attention. These anecdotal reports once again reveal the carelessness or unpreparedness of some journalists for encounters with Asian American newsmakers. This finding suggests the possibility of many more misreported stories that remain uncorrected and others that have simply been framed in a stereotypical fashion.

Likely starting in the 1980s, the "model minority" images of Asian Americans began to take shape in mass media. A *New Republic* article uncovered many successful stories of Asian Americans who are self-sufficient and persevere during hard times (Bell, 1985). However, one can easily argue that this image can be a double-edged sword to Asian Americans. As pointed out by Dalisay (2006), Asian Americans are portrayed as closer to the Whites in American society, which may create resentment among other minorities and which also may deprive Asian Americans of the assistance other minorities receive in education and employment. Some poverty-stricken communities of Hmongs, Laotians, and Vietnamese are not getting the help they have long deserved. To some Asian American groups, this "model minority" image is far from the truth and has hindered them in their attempt to gain broad acceptance as citizens.

We argue that media images of Asian Americans are produced mainly by non-Asian Americans and wield great symbolic power, but have little to do with how Asian Americans perceive themselves. Here we borrow a concept from Hall (1997), who states that symbolic power is exercised through representational practices. We agree with the claimed magnitude and capacity of symbolic power, yet it seems crucial for us to extend our analysis to examine real power via symbolic power. Real power may be embodied in a wide variety of forms and practices; however, in democratic societies, it belongs to politics.

We also argue that only when Asian Americans are treated fairly in American culture, especially in media, will they have a fair opportunity to hold public offices, exercise their power in the political arena, and participate fully in political discourse. Consequently, we focused our research efforts on exploring the ways in which Asian American politicians have pursued electoral victory in several states, how the media have treated this new and novel breed of politicians, how the public has responded to Asian American candidates, and what campaign veterans have to say about the races—their thoughts, strategies, and recollection of crucial events.

Our study also may be considered an example of Asian American political participation in the context of media, communication, and public perception. Scholars have described Asian Americans, at least until recently, as a people of political quiescence, with a lower percentage of the population being registered to vote than other races and ethnicities in the United States, let alone actually voting, running campaigns, and fielding candidates for public office (Lien, 1997, 2001; Lien et al., 2001, 2004). The Asian American population, despite its fast growth rate and impressive level of average education, income, and professional achievement, has been overlooked by studies of minority politics (Lai, Cho, Kim, & Takeda, 2001). Few studies of minority politics have included Asian Americans, and few policymakers who advocate fairness in social issues and address discrimination have mentioned Asian Americans in their arguments for social justice. For historical, cultural, and institutional reasons, the Asian American minority has not been as vocal, proactive, and forceful with their political rights and perspectives as other racial or ethnic groups in the United States (Aoki & Nakanishi, 2001).

In the mid-19th century, Chinese laborers contributed significantly to the construction of transcontinental railroads. Later, a good number of Japanese farmers immigrated to Hawaii and the West Coast. Yet descendents of immigrants from Japan in the early 20th century and recent immigrants from India and the Philippines share no commonality in language, religion, or history of settlement and assimilation in the United States. Immigration and naturalization laws that unfairly favored European immigrants were practiced in the United States until 1965 (Aoki & Nakanishi, 2001). Once these discriminatory laws were annulled, immigration from Asia increased dramatically. The ethnic group label *Asian American* is an artificial construct arising from a need for a U.S. Census demographic classification, and it remains "a category in flux" (Aoki & Nakanishi, 2001, p. 605). It was not until the final two decades of the 20th century that the term *Asian American* even existed in common language.

As argued earlier, it is problematic to characterize as cohesive and homogenous an ethnic group whose diverse members have so little in common, and this problem has grown larger and more complicated as immigration from Asia has increased over the past 40 years. Therefore, special care must be taken to define what we mean by Asian American. The definition of *Asian American* and the many ethnic groups that are currently included under this umbrella has changed a number of times in the U.S. history. Whatever the definition, however, the label *Asian American* is inherently artificial, imposing, and subject to critique. Therefore, without the intent of endorsing it, this book simply uses the official (U.S. Census Bureau, 2002) definition of Asian American (i.e., all Americans whose ancestors came from the Asia-Pacific region, including Hawaii and Okinawa, all the way to South Asia, including India and Pakistan) for the purpose of studying this group of Americans. Diverse though they may be, resembling one another less than most other groups with whom they share minority status in the United States, it is apparent that this group of Americans has grown significantly in the past few decades and is understudied (with a few noted exceptions, many of which are cited in this book) in terms of their media representation and political participation. Without the scholarly study of this substantial group of citizens, the phenomena of mediated politics and minority involvement in the political process cannot be fully understood. This book aims to bridge this gap in the existing literature.

Previous studies have provided rich insights and explanations of Asian American lives in a historical context; this book is not intended to tread on the same trail. Instead, we are interested in exploring new avenues toward increased Asian American participation and visibility via the mass media and political platforms. We expect—and have observed— new generations of Asian Americans walking out of Chinatowns and Little Tokyo's and appearing confident and proactive in their embrace of media and politics in mainstream America. We seek to discover and understand new and successful paths for this emerging generation.

STRUCTURE OF THIS BOOK

Because each chapter addresses a different facet of our general topic, we understand some readers might choose to read only individual chapters.

Therefore, we have made a conscious decision to adopt a format that resembles a collection of all-inclusive, self-contained research articles, which is less common in books. Hence, literature is repeatedly mentioned in various chapters, and references follow each chapter, instead of appearing together at the end of the book.

Nevertheless, we strongly encourage our readers to read all chapters to obtain a comprehensive picture and a deeper understanding of the issues. For instance, if you only read chapters 3 or 5, you may or may not fully agree with our argument that the news media's mention of an Asian American candidate's ethnicity would likely have a negative impact on his or her race. We hope the hard evidence from the experiment reported in chapter 7 convinces you. At the same time, you may want to read chapter 6 to see what candidates and their campaign staff think of certain treatments by the news media.

Here is a preview of all the chapters. In American democracy, voting, public opinion, and the media are inextricably intertwined. In chapter 2, we assess the attitudes of the American people toward Asian Americans and seek to ascertain whether media exposure, along with other factors, can predict the American people's perceptions of Asian Americans. As discussed previously, there are many stereotypical images of Asian Americans that have become ingrained in Americans' minds, and the media are often the sole source of such stereotypes. Asian American images in the mass media are still rare, formulaic, and far more negative than images of Whites. Asian American candidates may be suffering at the affective level, if not at the rational level, in all kinds of political campaigns due to mass media's negative influence. In this chapter, we analyze survey data from American National Election Studies (NES) to examine the relationship between media use and attitudes toward Asian Americans. Also, we compare how various races use different kinds of media. The findings are useful for locating the origin of mediated influence on racial perceptions.

In chapter 3, we examine the ways in which Asian American candidates are presented to voters by the news media. This chapter analyzes media coverage of several prominent Asian Americans who ventured onto the campaign trail between 1993 and 2003, and it includes landmark races that amassed more than parochial electorate attention. We believe that only through systematic and thorough investigation of media coverage can we achieve a better understanding of the issues, discourse, and imagery in the campaigns of the Asian American candidates. Our quantitative content analysis includes the Michael Woo–Richard Riordan contest, both vying for Los Angeles mayor in 1993; Gary Locke versus Ellen Craswell for Washington governor in 1996; David Wu versus Molly

Bordonaro for Oregon's first Congressional district in 1998; California's Matt Fong versus Barbara Boxer 1998 battle for a seat in the U.S. senate; and, last, Piyush "Bobby" Jindal versus Kathleen Blanco for Louisiana governor in 2003.

We excluded political campaigns in Hawaii because Asian Americans are not a minority there. Such campaigns would be far less likely to demonstrate the challenges that face Asian American candidates in contests against non-Asians in the more "typical" campaigns conducted on the U.S. mainland. In states other than Hawaii, it is absolutely necessary for Asian American office seekers to reach out to other ethnic minorities or the majority group because there are simply not enough Asian American votes to carry an election, even in the unlikely event that they vote as a cohesive group. Except for the Woo and Wu cases, the Asian American candidates all needed to conduct comprehensive statewide campaigns to have a chance at being elected.

Given the influence of media on politics, the forces that drive the media's coverage and presentation of ethnic minorities interest numerous researchers. Ethnicity-conscious scholars and industry critics have often argued and advocated for a larger presence of minorities in both media content and the media workplace. Chapter 4 seeks to verify the conventional wisdom that the presence of ethnic journalists—Asian Americans, in this case—results in more and better coverage of ethnic groups. Eight newspapers are analyzed, including those representative of communities with varying numbers of Asian Americans as well as papers from geographic regions across the nation. The study concludes that newspapers with more Asian American staff members generate more stories about, and thus broader community coverage of, Asian Americans. Likewise, newspapers in cities with larger Asian American populations are more likely to have more Asian American staff members and to provide more coverage of Asian Americans. However, the impact of Asian American staff on news coverage is found to be stronger than the influence of Asian American populations. The influences of Asian American journalists can be found in sourcing, substance, and context of stories.

Chapter 5 is devoted to discussing the frames and underlying themes that reporters employ to describe these Asian American candidates, their campaigns, and the issues they face. We sought a more holistic approach by employing a strategy of triangulation in which multiple techniques are applied to more distinctly define the target phenomenon. The phenomenon is quite complex and our goal ambitious. Therefore, we not only need to examine the statistics of news coverage and public opinion, but also unveil the hidden messages and ideologically loaded terms delivered by journalists. Doing so leads to a better understanding of the total phenomenon and more knowledge about how reporters—perhaps, for the first time—tackled a political race between a non-Asian and Asian American candidate. Also in chapter 5, we hope to uncover the dominant themes and frames that consistently appear in media coverage across the races and to investigate which are effective for Asian American candidates and which are not. These lessons could be highly beneficial for aspiring Asian American office seekers.

In chapter 6, we report our analysis and findings from interviews of several prominent Asian American politicians, including Gary Locke, David Wu, and Matt Fong. We also include our analysis of interviews with the experienced political consultants who worked with these candidates. This series of in-depth inquiries sought to uncover the unique problems these campaign veterans faced and to reveal the particular media and campaign strategies they used to make their campaigns work.

We interviewed Blair Butterworth, a long-time consultant working with Gary Locke; Jeston Black, a member of David Wu's campaign staff during his first congressional campaign; and Luke Letlow, who ran Bobby Jindal's 2002 gubernatorial campaign and worked in Jindal's New Orleans office at the time of the interview. These interviews provided intriguing insights and unique perspectives that casual observers could hardly imagine. Last, we interviewed political reporters who covered these races. Their candid accounts helped shed considerable light on the races explored in this project. The perspectives and knowledge revealed through these qualitative analyses worked in concert with the quantitative methods we employed to triangulate the whole truth, developing a richer and deeper understanding of race, politics, the media.

In chapter 7, we employ yet another method of analysis by conducting a complex experiment that examines the relationship among a candidate's ethnic background, gender, and his or her perceived attributes and electability. In reality, it is almost impossible for researchers to encounter a situation where people of all colors and genders enter a race simultaneously. Yet it is important to compare the perceived attributes, and the odds of winning for candidates in different ethnic groups, thus necessitating controlled experimentation.

In response to the recurring validity concern regarding the use of college students as subjects in psychological experiments, we recruited staff members of Washington State University (WSU) and Louisiana State University (LSU), as well as their family members who were not students, to participate in this experiment. The fact that the two campuses are located in culturally and politically distinctive regions elevates the level of external validity of the sample. In addition, we examine the impact of demographic and psychological factors on subjects' assessments and preferences of fictional candidates with identical credentials and experiences. These findings may serve as a foundation for future investigation on the impact of demographics on perceived electability. The results demonstrate that race is an important factor in deciding voters' preference and that it is more decisive than gender.

Because each preceding chapter already has a conclusion, chapter 8, which is relatively short, consists of our closing thoughts and recommendations.

We aimed high when we commenced the research projects detailed in this book. Each campaign we investigated is unique; the context behind each election is different, and some of the scenarios we investigated might never happen again (as presented in chap. 7). These differences work to our advantage, however, as we hope to draw a more comprehensive, synthetic picture of ethnicity, politics, and media from various angles and points of view. We were passionate about studying these campaigns and the issues surrounding mediated politics for Asian Americans because no one in the past had ever systematically examined these topics at this scale.

Although we would disagree, one could argue that focusing on one ethnic group would place our research in the category of a *niche study*, a euphemism often used to describe research about which few people care. Yet after years of working in this area, we have grown even more enthusiastic about this project and its importance. After reading the following chapters, we are confident that you will have received a comprehensive and in-depth exposure to the major issues regarding media, politics, and Asian Americans today.

REFERENCES

Aoki, A. L., & Nakanishi, D. T. (2001). Asian Pacific Americans and the new minority politics. *PS: Political Science & Politics*, 605–610.

Bell, D. (1985, July 15). The triumph of Asian Americans. *The New Republic, 22*, 24–31.

Dalisay, F. S. (2006). *The implications of the Asian American "model minority" stereotype on perceptions of African Americans.* Unpublished master's thesis, Washington State University, Pullman, WA.

Fancher, M. R. (2002, March 3). Time won't forget readers' reminder on Kwan headline. *Seattle Times*, p. A2.

Feagans, B. (2006, December 11). "No Spanish on my dime"; English-only sentiment grows loud. *The Atlanta Journal-Constitution*, p. 1A.

Feng, P. X. (Ed.). (2002). *Screening Asian Americans*. New Brunswick, NJ: Rutgers University Press.

Ghymn, E. M. (2000). Asians in film and other media. In E. M. Ghymn (Ed.), *Asian American studies: Identity, images, issues past and present* (pp. 135–150). New York: Peter Lang.

Hall, S. (Ed.). (1997). *Representation: Cultural representations and signifying practices*. Thousand Oaks, CA: Sage.

Hamamoto, D. Y. (1994). *Monitored peril: Asian Americans and the politics of TV representation*. Minneapolis: University of Minnesota Press.

Hamamoto, D. Y., & Liu, S. (Eds.). (2000). *Countervisions: Asian American film criticism*. Philadelphia, PA: Temple University Press.

Har, J. (2007, January 27). GOP presses immigration; Democrats says "later." *The Oregonian*, p. A1.

Hinckley, D. (2005, April 29). Talk-show apologies: That's infotainment. *New York Daily News*. Retrieved April 29, 2005, from http://www.nydailynews.com

Isaacs, H. R. (1958). *Scratches on our minds: American images of China and India*. New York: John Day.

Kim, E. H. (1982). *Asian American literature: An introduction to the writings and their social context*. Philadelphia: Temple University Press.

Lai, J. (2000). *The recruitment of Asian Pacific American elected officials and their impact on group political mobilization*. Unpublished doctoral dissertation, University of Southern California, Los Angeles, CA.

Lai, J. S., Cho, W. K. T., Kim, T. P., & Takeda, O. (2001, September). Asian Pacific-American campaigns, elections, and elected officials. *PS: Political Science & Politics*, 611–617.

Lee, R. G. (1999). *Orientals: Asian Americans in popular culture*. Philadelphia, PA: Temple University Press.

Lee, W. H., & Zia, H. (2002). *My country versus me: The first-hand account by the Los Alamos scientist who was falsely accused of being a spy*. New York: Hyperion.

Lien, P. (1997). *The political participation of Asian Americans: Voting behavior in Southern California*. New York: Garland.

Lien, P. (2001). *The making of Asian American through political participation*. Philadelphia: Temple University Press.

Lien, P., Collet, C., Wong, J., & Ramakrishnan, S. K. (2001). Asian Pacific-American public opinion and political participation. *PS: Political Science and Politics*, 34(3), 625–630.

Lien, P., Conway, M. M., & Wong, J. (2004). *The politics of Asian Americans: Diversity and community*. New York: Routledge.

Lyke, M. L. (2001, May 24). Japanese Americans on alert for movie backlash. *Seattle Post-Intelligencer*, p. A1.

Paek, H. J., & Shah, H. (2003). Racial ideology, model minorities, and the "not-so-silent partner": Stereotyping of Asian Americans in U.S. magazine advertising. *Howard Journal of Communication*, 14(4), 225–243.

Referendum revelations. (2006, November 11). *Wall Street Journal*, p. A6.

Riccardi, N., & Gaouette, N. (2006, December 17). Employers' immigration pains; Recent raids illustrate a conundrum. *Los Angeles Times*, p. A37.

Signs of hope on immigration. (2006, November 20). *New York Times*, p. A22.

Taylor, C. R., Landreth, S., & Bang, H.-K. (2005). Asian Americans in magazine advertising: Portrayals of the "model minority." *Journal of Macromarketing, 25*(2), 163–174.

Taylor, C. R., & Stern, B. B. (1997). Asian Americans: Television advertising and the "model minority" stereotype. *Journal of Advertising, 26*(2), 47–61.

U.S. Census Bureau. (2002, February). *The Asian population 2000.* Retrieved March 12, 2007, from http://www.census.gov/prod/2002pubs/c2kbr01-16.pdf

Wong, E. F. (1978). *On visual media racism: Asians in the American motion pictures.* New York: Arno.

Wu, H. D. (1996). An enduring schema: The image of the Chinese in American prime time television dramas. *International Communication Gazette, 58,* 69–86.

Yip, A. (1997, June 13–15). *Remembering Vincent Chin: Fifteen years later, a murder in Detroit remains a turning point in the APA movement.* Retrieved March 10, 2007, from http://www.asianweek.com/061397/feature.html

Chapter 2

Mass Media and Public Attitudes Toward Asian Americans

In this chapter, we discuss three aspects about the media: media portrayals of Asian Americans, media-influenced attitudes toward Asian Americans, and media usage among Asian Americans. The multiple goals of this chapter are to examine possible connections between media exposure and attitudes toward this minority group, and to provide suggestions about how to reach Asian Americans via mass media.

Mass media's effects on audience beliefs and behaviors have attracted much scholarly attention. Many studies of this nature focus on audience attitudes that are based on racial stereotyping. Most of such research concerns media portrayals of African Americans and occasionally Hispanic Americans (e.g., Dixon & Linz, 2000; Entnam, 1990, 1994; Entman & Rojecki, 2000; Fujioka, 1999, 2005; Rada, 2000). By comparison, representation of Asian Americans in the media is rare, and communication scholars have paid relatively little attention to the portrayal of this group of citizens.

With cultivation and uses and gratifications as the theoretical framework (Holbert, Kwak, & Shah, 2003), this chapter uses a large, bi-annual national survey (National Election Studies) to gauge public attitudes toward Asian Americans, and to investigate the potential linkage between audience usage of various media and their attitudes toward this minority group. Considering the scanty and stereotypical representations of Asian Americans in news and entertainment media, as well as the dearth of communication research on this racial group, whether and how media consumption may affect public attitudes toward Asian Americans is a topic worth researching. A better understanding of this topic is beneficial to society at large and also may fill a void in media stereotyping research that traditionally focuses on African Americans.

In addition, with the same data, we examine media usage patterns among the five major racial/ethnic groups in the United States. This information has the potential to aid social marketers and political strategists in reaching Asian Americans to encourage their political participation.

ASIAN AMERICANS IN THE MEDIA

Scholars have established the scant and derogatory treatment of Asian Americans in the media (e.g., Auman & Mark, 1997; Hamamoto, 1994; Heuterman, 1997; Larson, 2006; R. Lee, 1999; Mansfield-Richardson, 1997; H. Wu & T. Lee, 2005). J. Lee (1994), for example, discovered that the largest number of news stories on Asian Americans was reported in connection to aspects of illegal immigration, crime, and gang violence. Two recent news story headlines implied that figure skating champion Michelle Kwan was not an American. When she lost in two competitions, instead of using a phrase such as "fellow American," news headlines read "American Beats Out Kwan" and "American Outshines Kwan" (Fancher, 2002; Lyke, 2001). Nuclear scientist Wen Ho Lee was wrongly accused by the government and news media of being a Chinese spy (W. Lee & Zia, 2002). In the 1990s, the news media helped promote the view that some Asian Americans, such as John Huang, were agents of foreign governments aiming to illegally influence U.S. politicians ("Campaign Finance," 1998; R. Lee, 1999; E. Liu, 1998).

In the entertainment media, Asian Americans have not fared well either. On the rare occasions when they appear on stage, in films, or TV shows, this group of Americans usually play either insignificant or stereotypical roles such as restaurant waiters, gangsters, or prostitutes who are incapable of integration or Americanization or are distorted into an "honorary" Whiteness (Eng, 2001; Larson, 2006; Shimakawa, 2002; H. Wu, 1996). The problem of such stereotypes has roots in historical, economic, and political dimensions (Hamamoto, 1994; Isaacs, 1958; Jones, 1955; Seiter, 1986; F. Wu, 2002).

These overwhelmingly negative media images associated with Asian Americans are likely to create doubts and ambivalence about them among other racial groups. This type of portrayal is possibly one of the reasons that Asian Americans are often perceived as "perpetual foreigners" despite their long history of residence in this country.

MEDIA USAGE AND EFFECTS ON ATTITUDES

Two communication theories and research approaches regarding media usages and effects were chosen as the theoretical framework of the present study. In essence, cultivation analysis theorizes that heavy TV use may lead to believing in the reality constructed by the media industry (Gerbner, 1998; Gerbner et al., 1978, 1979, 1980; Severin & Tankard, 1997). According to cultivation scholars, because of the frequent representation of violence on the TV screen, heavy viewers may perceive the world as cruel and frightening. Therefore, they tend to overestimate both the chance of being victimized and the number of people involved in law enforcement and crimes. They also are more likely to consider their fellow citizens untrustworthy. Although most cultivation literature focuses on TV viewing, other media were found to cultivate such attitudes as well (Severin & Tankard, 1997; Signorielli & Morgan, 1990).

Cultivation analysis, at least the earlier versions, assumes that audiences are passively influenced by media content. The uses and gratifications approach is based on an opposite premise. It aims to explain why, how, where, and when people consume specific media. Specific social and psychological needs or motives of audience members help determine their media consumption (Blumler & Katz, 1974; Rubin & Perse, 1987; Severin & Tankard, 1997). For example, sensation-seeking, aggressive, and alienated teenagers are attracted to violent film, Internet, and computer content (Slater, 2003).

The insights from both theories helped conceptualize the fundamental research question of this chapter: Regardless of whether the audience is passively influenced by the media or actively seeking certain content to fulfill their needs, is there a connection between media consumption and attitudes toward Asian Americans? Specifically, does media consumption contribute to pro- or anti-Asian American attitudes? Also, are people holding such attitudes more likely to use certain media? In addition, are there other characteristics of the audience that would affect their choice of media as well as their attitudes toward Asian Americans? To help the reader better understand the formation of these questions, more studies on media coverage of—and people's attitudes toward—minorities are reviewed here.

Negative portrayals of minority populations seem to be the norm in the mainstream media in the United States (Lester, 1996). Reviewing the media's portrayals of African Americans, Entman and Rojecki (2000) argued that both news and entertainment media constructed Blacks as inferior in many ways and helped shape White Americans' ambivalent attitudes toward them. Valentino (1999) reported that the news media's stereotypic portrayals of minorities could activate racial attitudes, which may subsequently affect voters' evaluations of political candidates.

According to Busselle and Crandall (2002), only a few studies have investigated the true linkage between media exposure and perception toward minorities, but its existence has been supported. For example, a higher level of attention to news on race relations may lead to a perception that greater socioeconomic disparities exist between Whites and African Americans and also is positively related to the belief that such difference is likely due to discrimination and lack of job opportunities (Gandy & Baron, 1998). Viewing entertainment programs on TV is related to the belief that Blacks are more successful than Whites, but news viewing may lead to the contrary perception (Armstrong et al., 1992). Participants in an experiment were found more likely to decide that a Black perpetrator in a news story was "lazy" and displayed a "lack of intelligence" than a White perpetrator (Gilliam & Iyengar, 1998).

In addition, Busselle and Crandall (2002) found that watching different genres of TV programs (drama, sitcom, and news) influences respondents' estimates of the income and education of White and African Americans, as well as possible reasons behind such achievements. News viewing is positively related to the belief that lack of motivation results in socioeconomic differences between Blacks and Whites. Watching sitcoms is positively related to the education and income level of African Americans. TV drama viewing predicts the perceptions that Whites are better educated than African Americans (Busselle & Crandall, 2002).

Studies in this line of research have produced useful information. However, at least three related areas have yet to be fully investigated. First, racial minorities' education, income, and involvement with crime seem to be the foci among studies of this nature, but the general public's overall political attitudes toward a specific minority group should be explored as well. Second, as F. Wu (2002) pointed out, there are other colors beyond Black and White in U.S. society and politics. The relationship between media usage and perceptions of Asian Americans also deserves some scrutiny from media scholars. Third, news is treated as a broad genre in some of the studies reviewed earlier. However, considering the ideological differences between news media in the United States, such as the fact that network news tends to be relatively centrist and political talk radio is overwhelmingly conservative, finer distinctions between the news media programs seem necessary. The present study seeks to shed some light on the three areas mentioned before.

PUBLIC ATTITUDES TOWARD ASIAN AMERICANS

Among all minorities in the United States, Asian Americans seem to be rather powerless. Until a few decades ago, most Asian Americans were confined in segregated ghettos in large cites, and their choice of profession and chance of promotion were limited. The Chinese Exclusion Act was not repealed until 1943, resulting in an annual quota of 105 Chinese immigrants. During World War II, Japanese Americans were sent to internment camps because their "mother country" was at war with the United States, even though their European American counterparts did not receive the same treatment (Tung, 1974; J. Wu & Song, 2000). The Korean and Vietnam Wars that followed probably increased the public's negative perception of Asian Americans. The increasing afflu-ence of some Asian countries in the 1980s and 1990s also made some Americans worry about the influence from Asia, which triggered frosty public sentiment toward Asian Americans. Likely due to such reasons, rates of hate crimes against Asian Americans were high during those two decades (R. Lee, 1999).

A reasonable explanation of such negative treatments is that Asian Americans are perceived as perpetual foreigners or outsiders. Although more Asian Americans are holding public office (Aoki & Nakanishi, 2001; Lai et al., 2001), this outsider status continues until today. In other words, many of their fellow citizens still do not perceive Asian Americans as "true" Americans (R. Lee, 1999; E. Liu, 1998; F. Wu, 2002). In a recent survey cosponsored by the Anti-Defamation League, 25% of the interviewed Americans hold strong negative views toward Chinese Americans. Also, 23% of Americans would not want a Chinese American to be the president, and 7% would not work for an Asian American CEO (Anti-Defamation League, 2001).

Despite much research on discrimination against Asian Americans in history, few studies are found on current public attitudes toward Asian Americans. Ho and Jackson (2001) contributed to this small body of knowledge by using college student samples to develop an Attitude Toward Asians (ATA) scale. Godfrey, Richman, and Withers (2000) took a similar approach and generated a 50-item scale to measure stereotypes, prejudice, and discrimination toward a variety of ethnic, religious, and sexual groups, including Asian Americans. He (2002) conducted a local survey in Austin, Texas, to measure residents' attitudes toward skilled Asian immigrants. We could not find studies that have reported representative public attitudes toward Asian Americans in general. A recent and notable exception is the 2001 national survey cosponsored by the Anti-Defamation League and the Committee of 100 (a group of prominent Chinese Ameri-cans) mentioned earlier. They claimed that it was the first opinion poll of its kind. The linkage between media and American attitudes toward Asian Americans, nevertheless, was not addressed in the survey.

RACES AND ETHNICITIES IN RESEARCH OF MEDIA USE

Before turning to our investigation, it is imperative to survey common categories of races and ethnicities in the country. There are arguments about the construct of the Hispanic/Latino/Chicano group, which appears to be the result of governmental labeling, rather than a self-described group identity (U.S. Census Bureau, 2001). Recent consensus suggests that this group's commonality is more about language than about race. Thus, a Hispanic can be a Spanish-speaking White, Black, Asian, or any combination of different races. Nevertheless, this group is commonly treated as a single racial/ethnic group in government-sponsored and academic surveys, including the National Election Studies (NES), which identifies five major racial/ethnic groups in the United States: African Americans, Asian Americans, Hispanic/Latino Americans, Native Americans, and Caucasian Americans. Within broader racial groups, there also are subcategories of ethnic groups (e.g., Korean Americans and Japanese Americans). Ethnicity usually has roots in race, national origin, and cultures (Subervi-Velez, 1986), making it far more difficult to define. The present study adopts the common definitions and focuses on the five racial/ethnic groups.

Communication scholars have reported differences in media use among both adults and children across various races and ethnicities (Comstock, Chaffee, Katzman, McCombs, & Roberts, 1978; Dorr, 1986; Shoemaker, 1984). For instance, African American adults are found to watch a large amount of TV (Bush et al., 1999). Few studies, however, have presented exact differences across racial/ethnic groups (Blosser, 1988). Also, all of the aforementioned studies were conducted before 2000, which might make their findings a bit outdated given the drastic and rapid changes in American demographics. Therefore, an updated study seems needed to fill the gap.

As discussed earlier, many studies of this nature have focused on the difference between African Americans and Whites (e.g., Bush et al., 1999; Comstock et al., 1978; Greenberg & Brand, 1994). A few of the media usage studies included Latino samples. For example, Allen and Clark (1980) compared the use of broadcast and print media between African Americans and several Latino groups (Chicanos, Puerto Ricans, and Cubans). Another study by Greenberg and his colleagues (1983) examined the differences between White and Mexican American children and adults in terms of their use of broadcast and print media. Little literature exists on empirical investigations that deal with Asian or Native Americans.

DIFFERENCES IN MEDIA USAGE ACROSS RACIAL GROUPS

According to the literature (Blosser, 1988; Bush et al., 1999; Comstock et al., 1978; Newhagen, 1994; Pearl, Bouthilet, & Lazar, 1982), both African American children and adults were found to watch more TV than their White counterparts. Greenberg and Brand (1998) noted that most research examined exposure to TV entertainment programs instead of TV news. They also found that Blacks watch less TV news than Whites.

Black consumers reportedly listen to the radio more often than Whites (Blosser, 1988). As a result, radio was proclaimed an ideal medium to reach African Americans (Legette, 1994; Stark, 1993). According to Greenberg and his coauthors (1983), there was little difference between Latino and White consumers in terms of their exposure to entertainment programming or national and local TV news. Rather, a person's other demographic characteristics, including sex, age, income, and education, were better predictors of how much TV viewing took place (Greenberg et al., 1983). They also reported little difference in radio usage between these two groups.

A few studies (e.g., Newhagen, 1994) reported little difference in newspaper use across race lines. However, in an earlier study, Weber and Fleming (1984) found that newspapers were a popular choice among Black youth, which could be questionable now because overall American youth are less likely to read or subscribe to newspapers (Stevenson, 1994). In addition, according to other studies (Bogart, 1972; Greenberg & Brand, 1998; Greenberg et al., 1983), Whites expose themselves more to print media than Blacks or Latinos do. Greenberg and his colleagues (1983, 1998) also found that newspaper readership was especially low among predominantly Spanish-speaking consumers: Only 45% of surveyed Latino consumers were regular newspaper readers while 30% were nonreaders. In comparison, the ratio of readers versus nonreaders was 68% to 12% among Whites (Greenberg & Brand, 1998).

Little research was conducted on Asian Americans' use of media. A book by Mansfield-Richardson (2000) includes a thorough review of a few existing studies. Surveys cited in this book have shown that Asian American consumers preferred TV and newspapers to radio or magazines. Also, various studies concurred that newspapers played an important role for Asian Americans' political knowledge (Chaffee, Nass, & Yang, 1990; Gall & Gall, 1993; Mansfield-Richardson, 2000). However, there were certain discrepancies between ethnic groups (e.g., Chinese vs. Vietnamese Americans) within the Asian American community.

Although existing studies on media use across racial/ethnic groups in the United States have provided valuable information, overall this line of research has been rather sporadic and less than systematic. African Americans are more likely than other minority groups to be the counterparts of Whites when researchers investigated the differences between races. Media use among Asian Americans and Native Americans was rarely addressed. Furthermore, the media examined in existing studies are far from representative of the commonly used media today—most such studies included newspapers or entertainment TV, but few addressed the Internet. Thus, the need for a new, systematic investigation is obvious.

Based on the existing—and scanty for certain groups—literature on comparative media use among races/ethnicities, it is difficult to formulate research hypotheses. Therefore, a research question would be more suitable under these circumstances. The last research question of the present study is whether there are noticeable, significant differences among racial groups in media usage.

HYPOTHESIS AND RESEARCH QUESTIONS

Four research questions and one hypothesis were formulated for this chapter:

RQ1: What are the general attitudes among Americans (regardless of their races and ethnicities) toward Asian Americans?

H1: Media usage in general is not a strong predictor of consumers' attitudes toward Asian Americans.

Rationale: Previous research has shown that Asian Americans' representations in the media are rare. Therefore, media usage should not predict consumers' overall attitudes toward this minority group.

RQ2: What are the best predictors of attitudes toward Asian Americans?

RQ3: Is the usage of certain media related to attitudes toward Asian Americans?

RQ4: How do Asian Americans differ from other groups of citizens in terms of their media usage? If social marketers and political strategists want to reach Asian Americans, which media should they use?

METHOD

The NES is widely used in political science and political communication research. This series of surveys has been conducted every other year by the Survey Research Center at the University of Michigan. It usually includes about 2,000 respondents randomly drawn from across the nation. Useful measures concerning attitudes toward Asian Americans existed only in recent years (1992, 1994, 2000, and 2002). These four NES datasets were used in the present study. To examine possible relationships between racial attitudes and media usage, the 2000 dataset—comprised of 1,807 respondents—was selected.

In the 2000 data, demographic independent variables include age, sex (dummy variable of male), race (dummy variable of White), income, and education. Other control variables that could affect respondents' racial attitudes include political ideology (liberal to conservative), partisanship (Democratic, Independent, or Republican), religiosity, political interest, internal efficacy, external efficacy, political cynicism (trust in government and democracy), support for equality, and pro-African American stance. It is common knowledge in U.S. politics that anti-immigrant and White supremacist attitudes are associated with political ideologies, partisanship, and religion. Because ideology can be broadly defined as a general worldview (Hinich & Munger, 1994), the last two variables can be viewed as being related to one's political ideology. In fact, these two factors likely have strong implications on political issues such as affirmative action and women's status. Factors including political interest, efficacy, and cynicism could affect one's political attitude in general and media usage. Therefore, these variables were controlled in the analysis.

Media-related independent variables included trust in media, how often respondents use national TV news, early local TV news, late local TV news, newspapers, morning TV news shows, daytime TV talk shows, political talk radio, and whether respondents have access to the Internet. Variables measuring attention to various media for the 2000 presidential campaigns (national TV news, local TV news, newspaper, and talk radio) were excluded.

In the 2000 survey, two variables related to Asian Americans were treated as dependent variables. One is the feeling thermometer on attitudes toward Asian Americans (v001327). This thermometer, with a range of 0–100, measures people's feelings about Asian Americans. Higher numbers mean a warmer and more positive attitude. The other dependent variable (v001440) is a scale measuring whether respondents feel that Asian Americans have too much (1), just about the right amount of (2), or too little (3) influence in politics. Although too little may not always be positive because to some people this could mean that Asian Americans can be disregarded, too much is definitely negative. Therefore, this can still be an acceptable measure of racial attitudes.

Due to the exploratory nature of this investigation, a stepwise method of multiple regressions was the method of choice. Only the final models were reported.

Media valuables also were analyzed using race as the grouping variable, and analysis of variance (ANOVA) procedures were run to compare media usage patterns across races. Because audiences' media habits can change rapidly, only recent (2000 and 2004) data are used for this part of analysis.

FINDINGS

Trends of Public Attitudes Toward Asian Americans

Regarding **RQ1**, Table 2.1 reveals that the public's feelings toward Asian Americans have improved since 1992. In 2000 and 2002, the feeling thermometer was way above the midpoint of 50. The percentage change between 1992 (mean = 56) and 2002 (mean = 63.32) is 13.6%. It should be noted, however, that only 339 people (13.6% out of 2,485) answered the thermometer question in 1992, compared with 1,265 (83.6% out of 1,513) in 2002. Also, because the mode of all 4 years is 50, Americans in general still seem rather ambivalent toward Asian Americans.

By comparison, African Americans have received higher thermometer ratings than Asian Americans. Hispanic Americans' general popularity, however, is not much different from that of Asian Americans. In 2000,

Table 2.1
Means of Feeling Thermometers Toward Asian Americans

| | Year | | | |
	1992	1994	2000	2002
Mean	56	60.29	65.48	63.32
Median	50	60	60	60
Mode	50	50	50	50
S.D.	20.53	18.72	19.65	19.26
N	339	730	1,417	1,265
Missing	2,146	1,065	390	248

the mean, median, and mode for Blacks are 67.48, 70, and 50, respectively (N = 1,452, S.D. = 20.91). For Hispanics, the figures are 64.32, 60, and 50 (N = 1,438, S.D. = 20.82). The mean, median, and mode for Blacks in 2002 are 66.28, 60, and 50, respectively (N = 1,246, S.D. = 19.16). For Hispanics they are 63.01, 60, and 50 (N = 1,256, S.D. = 19.79).

Predictors of Feeling Thermometer Ratings

Using the 100-degree, cold–warm feeling thermometer as the dependent variable, we found that the significant predictors are political interest, pro-African American stance, education, age, and external political efficacy (see Table 2.2). In other words, respondents would have a warmer feeling toward Asian Americans if they are interested in politics/campaigns (β = .17, p < .001), support policies favoring African Americans (β = .14, p < .001), are more educated (β = .09, p < .01), are younger (β = −.09, p < .01), and have more confidence in democracy and the political system (β = .09, p < .01). These are the answers to **RQ2**. No media related predictors turned out significant. Therefore, **H1** is supported.

Predictors of Beliefs of Asian Americans' Political Influence

When the dependent variable is whether respondents think Asian Americans have too much, about the right amount of, or too little influence and power in politics, significant predictors include: belief in equality, pro-African American stance, age, education, how many times respondents watch daytime talk shows like *Oprah*, and how many times they watch morning

Table 2.2
Predictors of Feelings Toward Asian Americans (N = 1,111)
(Fifth and Final Model)

Independent Variables	B	S.E.	β	p
Political interest	3.48	.66	.17	< .001
Pro-African Americans	3.06	.62	.14	< .001
Education	1.16	.39	.09	< .01
Age	−.11	.04	−.09	< .01
External efficacy	1.80	.64	.09	< .01
R-square = .10				

news shows like *Today* and *Good Morning America* (see Table 2.3). Respondents tend to believe that Asian Americans have too *little* influence if they are for equality ($\beta = .14$, $p < .01$), support pro-African American policies ($\beta = .14$, $p < .01$), are younger ($\beta = -.12$, $p < .01$), are better educated ($\beta = .08$, $p < .01$), are less religious ($\beta = -.06$, $p < .05$), are less likely to watch daytime TV talk shows ($\beta = -.08$, $p < .05$), but are more likely to watch morning news shows ($\beta = .07$, $p < .05$). These findings answer both **RQ2** and **RQ3**.

The first two items are easy to understand. If respondents support equality in general, and African Americans in particular, they also may support Asian Americans in obtaining more political power. The factors of education and age have been discussed earlier. But how do we explain the positive impact of viewing morning news shows and the negative impact of daytime talk shows? Except for a few programs, most daytime talk shows feature celebrity gossip or sensational stories, which may not appeal to a highly educated and open-minded audience. However, these people may choose to watch some morning TV news programs before leaving for work or school. Also, because the N (= 1,139) is rather large, one can argue that the cutoff point for statistical significance should be raised to .01. In this case, religiosity and all the media-related variables would be insignificant.

To answer **RQ3** in depth by performing further investigations of possible connections between media usage and attitudes toward Asian Americans, discriminant analysis with the stepwise method was executed to examine which media use variables can predict people's assessment of

Table 2.3
Predictors of Opinion of
Asian Americans' Political Influence ($N = 1{,}139$)
(Ninth and Final Model)

Independent Variables	B	S.E.	β	p
Equality	.10	.02	.14	< .001
Pro-African Americans	.09	.02	.14	< .001
Age	−.004	.001	−.11	< .001
Daytime talk shows	−.02	.01	−.07	< .05
Morning news shows	.01	.01	.07	< .05
Education	.03	.01	.08	< .01
Religiosity	−.03	.02	−.06	< .05
R-square = .11				

Table 2.4

A Discriminant Analysis of Predicting Evaluation
of Asian Americans' Political Influence (N = 1,408)

Used in Equation	Excluded From Equation
1. Daytime talk show	Days watching national TV news
2. Trust in media	Days watching early local TV news
3. Internet access	Days watching late local TV news
	Days reading newspaper
	Times watching morning news shows
	Listen to talk radio or not
	How often listen to talk radio

Note. Wilks' Lambda = 6.988, df = (6, 2806), p < .001.

Asian Americans' influence on politics (too much, about the right amount of, and too little). Of the 10 media-related variables, only three variables turned out to be significant: trust in media, time spent on daytime talk shows, and whether access to the Internet is available (see Table 2.4).

Based on Table 2.5, one can see the three variables function slightly differently in each of the three assessments. Persons who believe that Asian Americans have *too much* influence have the following profile: They trust the media less, are less likely than the other two groups to have Internet access, and watch more daytime talk shows. Those who

Table 2.5

Classification Function Coefficients* for Assessments of
Asian Americans' Political Influence

IV	Asian-Americans' Political Influence		
	Too much Influence (n = 82)	Just About the Right Amount (n = 576)	Too Little Influence (n = 750)
Daytime talk shows	.455	.255	.234
Trust in media	4.236	4.643	4.565
Internet access	2.503	3.231	3.563
(Constant)	−8.641	−7.825	−7.567

*Fisher's linear discriminant functions
Function 1: Canonical correlation = .161, x^2 = 41.645, df = 6, p < .001.
Function 2: Canonical correlation = .058, x^2 = 4.8, df = 2, p = .091.

believe that Asian Americans have *too little* influence have a different profile: They trust the media more than those who believe that Asian American have too much influence, but slightly less than those in the middle. Those individuals who belong to the *too little* group watch the least of daytime talk shows and are most likely to have Internet access. Therefore, according to this set of findings, the answer to **RQ3** is that Internet use and daytime talk shows viewing may predict attitudes toward Asian Americans, especially regarding their political influence.

It is important to note that the discriminant analysis does not control demographic variables such as age and education. However, the media use variables in the equation still disclose an interesting pattern. Those who believe that Asian Americans have *too much* influence have the lowest level of trust in media, which suggests that this group of people, perhaps out of their media use habit—such as watching too much daytime talk shows—are doubtful about what is presented in the news media. In addition, because of their lack of access to the Internet, they may have less exposure to diverse knowledge or alternative viewpoints.

Sample Sizes of Racial Groups

In the 2000 data, among the 1,746 cases analyzed, White Americans account for 79.8% of the sample ($n = 1,393$), followed by African Americans (11.9%; $n = 208$), Latinos (5.3%; $n = 93$), Asian Americans (1.8%; $n = 32$), and Native Americans (1.1%; $n = 20$). The 2004 data show a similar order of sizes. There are 1,177 respondents for analysis. Among them, 74.4% ($n = 876$) are White Americans, followed by African Americans (15.3%; $n = 180$), Latinos (6.9%; $n = 81$), Asian Americans (2.4%; $n = 28$), and Native Americans (1%; $n = 12$). The percentages of the surveyed respondents show that Latinos and Asian Americans are undersampled; in other words, they are below the percentages reported by the 2000 census.

Media Usage Across Races

Tables 2.6 and 2.7 report the means (of how many days a week) of exposure to various media. ANOVA and post-hoc Tukey tests were run to examine which two groups were significantly different. Next, the means were compared and translated into rankings, which are reported in Tables 2.8 and 2.9.

Figures in Tables 2.6 and 2.8 suggest that, in 2000, African Americans ranked number 1 in the viewing of both late local TV news and

Table 2.6
Media Exposures in a Week—2000 Data

Variable	National TV News	Early Local News	Late Local News	Newspapers	Morning News Shows on TV	Daytime Talk Shows
African Am.						
M	3.37	3.75	3.13[a]	2.61[a]	3.27[ab]	1.79[a]
SD	2.82	2.80	2.66	2.69	3.50	2.61
Asian Am.						
M	3.53	3.25	2.09	3.13	2.52	.84
SD	3.11	3.10	2.57	3.00	2.93	1.49
Native Am.						
M	3.80	2.90	2.65	3.70	2.94	1.88
SD	3.00	3.13	3.08	3.13	3.79	3.40
Latino Am.						
M	2.45[a]	3.03	2.70	2.51[b]	1.88[a]	1.18
SD	2.56	2.95	2.75	2.71	2.55	2.33
Caucasian Am.						
M	**3.32**[a]	**3.24**	**2.47**[a]	**3.64**[ab]	**2.40**[b]	**.78**[a]
SD	2.80	2.85	2.71	2.94	3.28	1.83
F (df = 4)	2.40*	1.74	2.98*	8.42***	3.12*	10.36***
N	1,742	1,745	1,744	1,745	1,474	1,475
Eta	.07	.06	.08	.14	.09	.17

Note. *p < .05. **p < .01. ***p <.001.
Means in the same column that share the same subscripts differ at p < .05.

Table 2.7
Media Exposures in a Week—2004 Data

Variable	National TV News	Early Local News	Late Local News	Newspapers	Online Newspapers
African Am.					
M	3.66	4.22[ab]	3.83[ab]	2.48[a]	.66
SD	2.63	2.66	2.70	2.67	1.70
Asian Am.					
M	4.61[a]	3.36	2.93	2.07	1.39
SD	2.63	2.92	2.51	2.52	2.41
Native Am.					
M	5.17[b]	4.08	4.42	2.83	1.00
SD	2.48	2.81	2.71	3.13	2.37
Latino Am.					
M	2.72[ab]	2.72[a]	2.49[a]	2.01[b]	1.12
SD	2.80	2.58	2.67	2.62	2.38
Caucasian Am.					
M	**3.57**	**3.08**[b]	**2.59**[b]	**3.33**[ab]	**.92**
SD	2.77	2.78	2.70	2.92	2.01
F (df = 4)	4.02**	7.46***	9.32***	7.44***	1.34
N	1,174	1,174	1,176	1,176	1,176
Eta	.12	.16	.18	.16	.07

Note. *p < .05. **p < .01. ***p <.001.
Means in the same column that share the same subscripts differ at p < .05.

Table 2.8
Rankings of Media Exposures—2000 Data

Variable	National TV News	Early Local News	Late Local News	Newspapers	Morning News Shows on TV	Daytime Talk Shows
African Am.						
Within media	4	1	1	4	1	2
Within race	*2*	*1*	*4*	*5*	*3*	*6*
Asian Am.						
Within media	2	2	5	3	3	4
Within race	*1*	*2*	*5*	*3*	*4*	*6*
Native Am.						
Within media	1	5	3	1	2	1
Within race	*1*	*3*	*5*	*2*	*4*	*6*
Latino Am.						
Within media	3	4	2	5	5	3
Within race	*4*	*1*	*2*	*3*	*5*	*6*
Caucasian Am.						
Within media	5	3	4	2	4	5
Within race	*2*	*3*	*4*	*1*	*5*	*6*

Table 2.9
Rankings of Media Exposures—2004 Data

Variable	National TV News	Early Local News	Late Local News	Newspapers	Online Newspapers
African Am.					
Within media	3	1	2	3	5
Within race	*3*	*1*	*2*	*4*	*5*
Asian Am.					
Within media	2	3	4	4	1
Within race	*1*	*2*	*3*	*4*	*5*
Native Am.					
Within media	1	2	1	2	3
Within race	*1*	*3*	*2*	*4*	*5*
Latino Am.					
Within media	5	5	5	5	2
Within race	*1*	*1*	*3*	*4*	*5*
Caucasian Am.					
Within media	4	4	3	1	4
Within race	*1*	*3*	*4*	*2*	*5*

morning news shows. They also ranked second for daytime talk shows. Data in Table 2.7 and 2.9 also reveal that African Americans ranked high (first and second, respectively) in early and late local news viewing in 2004. These findings are consistent with existing literature that African Americans tend to watch more TV (e.g., Bush et al., 1999). However, they are not leading in all TV viewing categories. In terms of national TV news, they are ranked only third or fourth among the five racial groups in both years.

Native Americans led in watching national TV news in both 2000 and 2004. For the same media category, Asian Americans ranked second in both years. Figures in all four tables show that White and Native Americans read newspapers more often than other racial/ethnic groups. Asian Americans were ranked third and fourth in both years for newspaper readership, which differs from existing literature reported earlier. Latinos ranked last in four media categories in 2004, but their rankings varied across media in 2000.

It is interesting to point out that of the six media categories examined in the 2000 survey, five of them result in significant difference among the races. Only the use of early local news among the groups is not statistically significant. The use of newspapers and daytime talk shows revealed the most discrepancies among the races (Eta = .14 and .17, respectively, see Table 2.6). For the 2004 data, one can see that all media types except for online newspapers resulted in significant differences in media usage between racial groups. The fact that the Internet is still a new medium could have contributed to its insignificant difference in usage.

Post-hoc Tukey test results reported in Tables 2.6 and 2.7 reveal that African Americans and White Americans differed in late local TV news viewing in both 2000 and 2004. In terms of newspaper reading, Whites and Blacks as well as Whites and Latinos differed in both years. Additionally, 2000 data (see Table 2.6) shows that African Americans watched significantly more morning news and daytime talk shows. These findings, coupled with an analysis of the means, also suggest that African Americans overall tend to watch more TV, and White Americans tend to reach newspapers more often.

Media Preferences Within Races and the Answer to RQ4

One also can look at Tables 2.8 and 2.9 to see each racial group's usage ranking among the media in each year. For example, in 2000, the order of Asian Americans' most used media is as follows: national TV news, early local TV news, newspapers, morning news shows on TV, late local news on TV, and daytime talk shows. The order in 2004 is as follows: national TV news, early local TV news, late local news, newspapers, and online daily newspapers. Data from both years indicate that Asian Americans rely mainly on TV for news, which answers RQ4. This pattern is similar to that found among Native Americans. Both African Americans and Latino Americans, however, seemed to rely heavily on early local news in both years.

These rankings do not differ much from those of White Americans. The order of media exposure among White Americans in 2000 was as follows: newspapers, national TV news, early local news, late local news, morning news shows on TV, and daytime talk shows. In 2004, their order was national TV news, newspapers, early local news, late local news, and online newspapers. Except for newspapers, the orders of media preferences between White and Asian Americans are similar.

In both years, the media habits of Asian and Native Americans are somewhat similar. For instance, in 2000, their rankings of national TV news, morning news shows on TV, and daytime talk shows were identical. Latino and Asian Americans' patterns of media exposure were different in 2000. However, in 2004, their rankings of media usage were almost identical. This set of comparisons suggests that similarities exist between races.

Tests of nonparametric correlation also were performed on the means of media uses reported in Tables 2.6 and 2.7. In 2000, only Asian Americans and Native Americans were correlated in their media usage rankings (Spearman's rho = .83, p < .05). In 2004, Asian Americans' media use correlates well with that of Native Americans (Spearman's rho = .90, p < .05) and Latinos (Spearman's rho = .98, p < .01). These findings further demonstrate the differences of media use among racial groups.

The Issue of a Potential Knowledge Gap

Online access to information could be a potential source of the knowledge gap between races because it involves computers, new technologies, and more expensive services from telephone or cable companies. Unfortunately, the data about reading daily newspapers online in 2004 did not lead to findings with statistical significance. Perhaps the survey question, which focuses exclusively on access to online newspapers, is too narrowly defined. However, a dichotomous (yes vs. no) measure of online access across races revealed important information.

The two cross-tabulations presented in Tables 2.10 and 2.11 suggest that African Americans have the lowest within-group ratios of Internet

Table 2.10
Internet Access by Race—2000 Data

Variable	African Am.	Asian Am.	Native Am.	Latino Am.	White Am.	Total
Have access (N)	66	18	10	42	803	939
Column %	40.7%	72%	62.5%	60.9%	65%	
Don't have (N)	96	7	6	27	432	568
Column %	59.3%	28%	37.5%	39.1%	35%	
Total	162	25	16	69	1,235	1,507

$\chi^2 = 37.02$, $df = 4$, $p < .001$.

access. In 2000, only 40.7% of African Americans had such access. Although the percentage increased to 60.5% in 2004, they were still the lowest in comparison with other races. In both years, Asian Americans ranked the highest, followed by White Americans, and Native Americans were in the middle (third). Latinos ranked fourth in 2000 and third (tied) in 2004.

CONCLUSION AND DISCUSSION

Overall, the general public's attitudes toward Asian Americans are weakly positive and have improved since the early 1990s. Such progress seems to correspond with this group's increasing visibility and influence in U.S. politics in the past decade. Also, media usage in general appears to have little connection with such attitudes.

Table 2.11
Internet Access by Race—2004 Data

Variable	African Am.	Asian Am.	Native Am.	Latino Am.	White Am.	Total
Have access (N)	95	16	7	47	577	742
Column %	60.5%	80%	70%	70%	73.9%	
Don't have (N)	62	4	3	19	204	292
Column %	39.5%	20%	30%	28.8%	26.1%	
Total	157	20	10	66	781	1,034

$\chi^2 = 12.23$, $df = 4$, $p < .01$; two cells (20%) have Ns smaller than 5.

Much literature suggests that racial stereotyping is common in mass media. Therefore, it is logical to suspect that media usage may lead to negative attitudes toward Asian Americans. Our findings do not entirely support this argument. The answer to the second research question is that media usage predicts attitudes toward Asian Americans in varied ways and that often the impact is intertwined with respondents' demographics and political attitudes.

As reported, media usage has no impact on the feeling thermometer variable. Instead, one's racial and political attitudes are the best predictors. When the dependent variable changed from general cold–warm feelings to a more concrete measure of Asian American's political influence, some media-related predictors became significant, at least arguably. However, individuals' racial and equality attitudes still have a stronger impact than media usage. Therefore, it can be argued that media usage contributes little to an audience members' attitudes toward a group of racial minority.

Why do our findings differ from the conclusion of many studies on media and racial attitudes? A few factors are probably at work. First, many previous studies relied on content analysis, which unveiled content trends that could not prove causal relationships. Second, for studies that did measure causal relationships, many exposed their experimental subjects to media content showing racial minorities. Other survey research used instruments containing many items about respondents' racial attitudes. Either way, participants were, or could be, primed to think about racial issues. In comparison, NES respondents were more likely to think about politics in general, rather than racial minorities during the survey. As a result, the power (the possibility of becoming significant predictors) of racial issues may be weaker in the present research in comparison with other studies. Third, because Asian Americans rarely appear in the media, media usage may have little to do with audiences' attitudes toward Asian Americans.

Most findings in this chapter are easy to understand, so there are only a few puzzles that need to be addressed. The outcome regarding daytime talk shows by no means suggests that homemakers, who may have more time to watch daytime talk shows than other audiences, tend to be bigots. It is reasonable to suspect that some viewers of "trashy" talk shows could be closed minded, but those who watch less sensationalistic shows like *Oprah* are more likely to hold progressive views. Second, many homemakers may not choose to watch TV during the day or may choose to watch other programs.

Why do people who watch morning news shows such as *Today* and *Good Morning America* tend to hold a more positive view toward Asian Americans? The content of those programs often has a national and international scope. Viewers interested in such information, and who make an effort to watch those shows in the morning, could be more open minded and in touch with changing social norms. In comparison, because local and national evening news broadcasts attract a broad audience, viewing these programs probably would not distinguish audience members' attitudes toward Asian Americans. Therefore, usage of other news media was not a significant predictor of racial attitudes.

In addition, as mentioned earlier in the findings, if the cutoff point for significance is raised from .05 to .01, *no* media-related variables would be significant predictors in our regression models.

It is somewhat of a surprise to us that newspaper readership did not turn out to be a significant predictor. Because reading requires more cognitive engagement, one may assume that newspaper readers are more intelligent and politically knowledgeable than users of other media (Y. Liu & Eveland, 2005) and, therefore, more supportive of Asian Americans. One possibility of the negative finding is that controlling other factors such as education and income somehow "balanced" or weakened its effect. Nevertheless, newspapers still did not survive in the discriminant analysis where extraneous factors were not held constant. In other words, like other media that attract a mass audience, newspapers may appeal to people holding various racial attitudes.

This particular finding is in fact good news for equality-minded activists because it means that all news media could be used to educate the public and promote racial harmony. If such educational messages appear in newspapers, and in local and national TV, they will reach people who hold unfavorable views of Asian Americans. In addition to ideas for a media campaign, there is another practical implication of the present study's findings. Activists promoting Asian American rights should work with African American and other minority organizations to promote equality for everyone.

Another set of findings in this chapter tells us what media are popular among Asian Americans. National and early evening TV news are the best vehicles to reach Asian Americans. Although the Internet does not rank high among Asian Americans, it is important to point out that, according to the 2004 data (Table 2.11), Asian Americans have the highest Internet access rate (80% have access vs. 20% without) among all five racial groups. This particular finding suggests that the Internet can be an effective way to reach Asian Americans.

This chapter has generated new and useful knowledge in three areas. First, as discussed earlier, public attitudes toward Asian Americans have rarely been reported in academic studies and the popular press. Although the data from 1992 and 1994 were not ideal due to the small numbers of respondents, the 2000 and 2002 surveys revealed representative public attitudes toward Asian Americans.

Second, this study is among the first to examine the relationship between general media usage and attitudes toward Asian Americans. Also, although a link has been established between media usage and negative attitudes toward African Americans in the existing literature (e.g., Entman & Rojecki, 2000), the present study suggests a different relationship between media consumption and attitudes toward Asian Americans. Scholars and activists interested in racial equality and harmony may find the findings of the present study useful for their future research and political campaigns.

Third, this chapter sheds light on media usages among all five racial groups in the United States in a systematic manner with recent survey data.

A minor technical issue to be discussed is the fact that the present study did not distinguish respondents' races in the analysis of thermometer ratings in Table 2.1. Some researchers may prefer to examine the attitudes of European Americans only or to exclude Asian Americans. However, because the first research question was about "public attitudes in general," the present authors decided not to exclude any racial groups.

Further studies are encouraged to address the limitations of the present study. Like all research using secondary data, the wording of some variables may not be ideal, and certain key variables could have been included. Therefore, future investigations may generate more, and more specific, questions measuring attitudes toward Asians Americans, as well as usage of more types of media. Items from the ATA scale and the survey sponsored by ADL and the Committee of 100 should be considered. Also, instead of broad categories of media, such as "daytime talk shows," it may be worthwhile to examine the effect of individual TV programs and other media vehicles. In addition, the impact of media usage on attitudes toward different races can be compared. Finally, the wording of questions about Internet access and sources was not ideal. More detailed questions about specific Internet venues should be used.

REFERENCES

Allen, R. L., & Clarke, D. E. (1980). Ethnicity and mass media behavior: A study of Blacks and Latinos. *Journal of Broadcasting, 24,* 23–34.

Anti-Defamation League. (2001, April 25). *American attitudes toward Chinese and Asian Americans.* Available at http://www.adl.org/misc/american_attitudes_towards_chinese.asp.

Aoki, A. L., & Nakanishi, D. T. (2001, September). Asian Pacific Americans and the new minority politics. *PS: Political Science & Politics,* 605–610.

Armstrong, B. G., Neuendorf, K. A., & Brentar, J. E. (1992). TV entertainment, news, and racial perceptions of college students. *Journal of Communication, 42*(3), 153–176.

Auman, A. E., & Mark, G. Y. (1997). The Chinese Americans. In A. D. Keever, C. Martindale, & M. A. Weston (Eds.), *U.S. news coverage of racial minorities* (pp. 191–215). Westport, CT: Greenwood.

Blosser, B. J. (1988). Ethnic differences in children's media use. *Journal of Broadcasting & Electronic Media, 32*(4), 453–470.

Blumler, J. G., & Katz, E. (Eds.). (1974). *The uses of mass communications: Current perspectives on gratifications research.* Beverly Hills, CA: Sage.

Bogart, L. (1972). Negro and White exposure: New evidence. *Journalism Quarterly, 49,* 15–21.

Brunner, B. et al. (2002). *Time Almanac 2003 with Information Please.* Boston: Information Please.

Bush, A. J., Smith, R., & Martin, C. (1999). The influence of consumer socialization variables on attitude toward advertising: A comparison of African-Americans and Caucasians. *Journal of Advertising, 28*(3), 13–24.

Busselle, R., & Crandall, H. (2002). Television viewing and perceptions about race differences in socioeconomic success. *Journal of Broadcasting & Electronic Media, 46*(2), 265–282.

Campaign Finance Key Player: John Huang. (1998). Retrieved on October 17, 2003, from http://www.washingtonpost.com/wp-srv/politics/special/campfin/players/huang.htm

Chaffee, S. H., Nass, C. I., & Yang, S. (1990). The bridging role of television in immigrant political socialization. *Human Communication Research, 17*(2), 266–288.

Comstock, G., Chaffee, S., Katzman, N., McCombs, M., & Roberts, D. (1978). *Television and human behavior.* New York: Columbia University Press.

Dixon, T. L., & Linz, D. (2000). Overrepresentation and underrepresentation of African Americans and Latinos as law breakers on television news. *Journal of Communication, 50*(2), 131–154.

Dorr, A. (1986). *Television and children: A special medium for a special audience.* Beverly Hills: Sage.

Eng, D. (2001). *Racial castration: Managing masculinity in Asian America.* Durham, NC: Duke University Press.

Entman, R. M. (1990). Modern racism and images of Blacks in local television news. *Critical Studies in Mass Communication, 7,* 332–346.

Entman, R. M. (1994). Blacks in television news: Television, modern racism and cultural changes. *Journalism Quarterly, 69*(2), 341–361.

Entman, R. M., & Rojecki, A. (2000). *The Black image in the White mind.* Chicago, IL: University of Chicago Press.

Fancher, M. R. (2002, March 3). Time won't forget readers' reminder on Kwan headline. *Seattle Times,* p. A2.

Fujioka, Y. (1999). Television portrayals and African-American stereotypes: Examination of television effects when direct contact is lacking. *Journalism & Mass Communication Quarterly, 76,* 52–75.

Fujioka, Y. (2005). Black media images as a perceived threat to African-American ethnic identity: Coping responses, perceived public perception, and attitudes toward Affirmative action. *Journal of Broadcasting & Electronic Media, 49,* 450–467.

Gall, S. B., & Gall, T. M. (Eds.). (1993). *Statistical record of Asian Americans.* Detroit, MI: Gale Research.

Gandy, O., Jr., & Baron, J. (1992). Inequality: It's all in the way you look at it. *Communication Research, 25*(5), 505–527.

Gandy, O., & Matabane, P. (1989). Television and social perceptions among African American and Hispanics. In M. K. Asante & W. B. Gudykunst (Eds.), *Handbook of international and intercultural communication* (pp. 318–348). Newbury Park, CA: Sage.

Gaziano, C. (1988, December). Community knowledge gaps. *Critical Studies in Mass Communication, 5,* 351–357.

Gaziano, C. (1997). Forecast 2000: Widening knowledge gaps. *Journalism & Mass Communication Quarterly, 74*(2), 237–264.

Gerbner, G. (1998). Cultivation analysis: An overview. *Mass Communication & Society 1*(3/4), 175–194.

Gerbner, G., Gross, L., Jackson-Beeck, M., Jeffries-Fox, S., & Signorielli, N. (1978). Television violence profile no. 9. *Journal of Communication, 28*(3), 176–207.

Gerbner, G., Gross, L., Morgan, M., & Signorielli, N. (1980). The "mainstreaming" of America: Violence profile no. 11. *Journal of Communication, 30*(3), 10–29.

Gerbner, G., Gross, L., Signorielli, N., Morgan, M., & Jackson-Beeck, M. (1979). The demonstration of power: Violence profile no. 10. *Journal of Communication, 29*(3), 177–196.

Gilliam, F. D., & Iyengar, S. (1998, August). *The corrosive influence of local television news on racial beliefs.* Paper presented to the annual meeting of the Association for Education in Journalism and Mass Communication, Baltimore, MD.

Godfrey, S., Richman, C. L., & Withers, T. N. (2000). Reliability and validity of a new scale to measure prejudice: The GRISMS. *Current Psychology: Developmental, Learning, Personality, Social, 19*(1), 3–20.

Greenberg, B. S., & Brand, J. E. (1994). Minorities and the mass media: 1970s to 1990s. In J. Bryant & D. Zillman (Eds.), *Media effects: Advances in theory and research* (pp. 273–314). Hillsdale, NJ: Erlbaum.

Greenberg, B. S., & Brand, J. E. (1998). U.S. minorities and the news. In Y. R. Kamalipour & T. Carilli (Eds.), *Cultural diversity and the U. S. media* (pp. 3–22). Albany: State University of New York Press.

Greenberg, B. S., Burgoon, M., Burgoon, J. K., & Korzenny, Z. F. (1983). *Mexican Americans and the mass media.* Norwood, NJ: Ablex.

Hamamoto, D. Y. (1994). *Monitored peril: Asian Americans and the politics of TV representation.* Minneapolis: University of Minnesota Press.

He, L. (2002 Spring). Perceptions, attitudes, and American public opinion toward skilled Asian immigrants. *University of Texas at Austin Undergraduate Research Journal, 1,* 10–22.

Heuterman, T. H. (1997). The Japanese Americans. In A. D. Keever, C. Martindale, & M. A. Weston (Eds.), *U.S. News coverage of racial minorities* (pp. 216–248). Westport, CT: Greenwood.

Hinich, M. J., & Munger, M. C. (1994). *Ideology and the theory of political choice.* Ann Arbor, MI: The University of Michigan Press.

Ho, C., & Jackson, J. W. (2001). Attitudes toward Asian Americans: Theory and measurement. *Journal of Applied Social Psychology, 31*(8), 1553–1581.

Holbert, R. L., Kwak, N., & Shah, D. (2003). Environmental concern, patterns of television viewing, and pro-environmental behaviors: Integrating models of media consumption and effects. *Journal of Broadcasting & Electronic Media, 47*(2), 177–196.

Isaacs, H. R. (1958). *Scratches on our minds: American images of China and India.* New York: John Day.

Jones, D. B. (1955). *The portrayal of China and India on the American Screen, 1896–1955.* Cambridge, MA: MIT Press.

Lai, J. S., Cho, W. K. T., Kim, T. P., & Takeda, O. (2001, September). Asian Pacific-American campaigns, elections, and elected officials. *PS: Political Science & Politics,* pp. 611–617.

Larson, S. G. (2006). *Media & minorities: The politics of race in news and entertainment.* Lanham, MD: Rowman & Littlefield.

Lee, J. (1994). A look at Asians as portrayed in the news. *Editor & Publisher, 127*(18), 56.

Lee, R. G. (1999). *Orientals: Asian Americans in popular culture.* Philadelphia, PA: Temple University Press.

Lee, W. H., & Zia, H. (2002). *My country versus me: The first-hand account by the Los Alamos scientist who was falsely accused of being a spy.* New York: Hyperion.

Legette, C. (1994). Key strategies for smart marketing to African Americans. *Public Relations Journal, 50*(7), 38–39.

Lemert, J. B. (1993). Do televised presidential debates help inform voters? *Journal of Broadcasting & Electronic Media, 37*(1), 83–94.

Lester, P. M. (Ed.). (1996). *Images that injure: Pictorial stereotypes in the media.* Westport, CT: Praeger.

Liu, E. (1998). *The accidental Asian: Notes of a native speaker.* New York: Random House.

Liu, Y., & Eveland, W. P., Jr. (2005). Education, need for cognition, and campaign interest as moderators of news effects on political knowledge: An analysis of the knowledge gap. *Journalism and Mass Communication Quarterly,* 910–929.

Lyke, M. L. (2001, May 24). Japanese Americans on alert for movie backlash. *Seattle Post-Intelligencer,* p. A1.

Mansfield-Richardson, V. (1997). In A. D. Keever, C. Martindale, & M. A. Weston (Eds.), *U.S. News coverage of racial minorities* (pp. 249–259). Westport, CT: Greenwood.

Mansfield-Richardson, V. (2000). *Asian Americans and the mass media: A content analysis of twenty United States newspapers and a survey of Asian American journalists.* New York: Garland.

Newhagen, J. E. (1994). Media use and political efficacy: The suburbanization of race and class. *Journal of the American Society for Information Science, 45*(6), 386–394.

Pearl, D., Bouthilet, L., & Lazar, J. (Eds.). (1982). *Television and behavior: Ten years of scientific progress and implications for the eighties, Vol. 1.* Summary Report (DHHS Publication No. ADM 82-1195). Washington, DC: U.S. Government Printing Office.

Rada, J. A. (2000). A new piece of the puzzle: Examining effects of television portrayals of African Americans. *Journal of Broadcasting & Electronic Media, 44*(4), 704–715.

Rubin, A. M., & Perse, E. M. (1987). Audience activity and television news gratifications. *Communication Research, 14,* 58–84.

Seiter, E. (1986). Stereotypes and the media: A re-evaluation. *Journal of Communication, 36*(2), 14–26.

Severin, W. J., & Tankard, J. W., Jr. (1997). *Communication theories: Origins, methods, and uses in the mass media.* New York: Longman.

Shimakawa, K. (2002). *National abjection: The Asian American body onstage.* Durham, NC: Duke University Press.

Shoemaker, P. (1984). *What do communication researchers really mean by "ethnicity?"* Paper presented at the International Communication Association convention, San Francisco.

Signorielli, N., & Morgan, M. (Eds.). (1990). *Cultivation analysis: New directions in media effects research.* Newbury Park, CA: Sage.

Slater, M. D. (2003). Alienation, aggression, and sensation seeking as predictors of adolescent use of violent film, computer, and website content. *Journal of Communication, 53*(1), 105–121.

Stark, P. (1993, January 4). Blacks attuned to radio. *Hollywood Reporter,* p. 27.

Stevenson, R. L. (1994). The disappearing newspaper reader. *Newspaper Research Journal, 15*(3), 22-31.

Subervi-Velez, F. A. (1986). The mass media and ethnic assimilation and pluralism: A review and research proposal with special focus on Hispanics. *Communication Research, 13,* 71–96.

Tung, W. (1974). *The Chinese in America.* Dobbs Ferry, NY: Oceana Publications.

U.S. Census Bureau. (2001, March). *Overview of Race and Hispanic Origin; Census 2000 Brief.* Retrieved on March 26, 2006, from <http://www.census.gov/prod/2001pubs/c2kbr01-1.pdf>

U.S. Census Bureau. (2003, April 17). *Asian Pacific American Heritage Month: May 2003.* Retrieved on March 26, 2006, from < http://www.census.gov/Press-Release/www/2003/cb03-ff05.html>

Valentino, N. A. (1999). Crime news and the priming of racial attitudes during evaluations of the president. *Public Opinion Quarterly, 63*(3), 293–320.

Weber, O. J., & Fleming, D. B. (1984). Black adolescents and the news. *The Journal of Negro Education, 53*(1), 85–90.

Wu, F. H. (2002). *Yellow: Race in America beyond black and white.* New York: Basic Books.

Wu, H. D. (1996). An enduring schema: The image of the Chinese in American prime time television dramas. *Gazette, 58,* 69–86.

Wu, H. D., & Lee, T. (2005). The submissive, the calculated, and the American Dream: Analyzing the news coverage of three Asian-American political candidates in the 1990s. *Howard Journal of Communications, 16*(3), 225–241.

Wu, J. Y. S., & Song, M. (2000). *Asian American studies: A reader.* New Brunswick, NJ: Rutgers University Press.

Chapter 3

News Coverage of
Asian American Candidates
1993–2003:
A Quantitative Analysis[1]

To any keen observer of U.S. politics, the voice and participation of Asian Americans have been rather inconspicuous. Few public office holders or political leaders at the state or federal levels are Asian descendents. If the elected politicians in Asian-dominant Hawaii were excluded, the picture of Asian Americans' political involvement in the nation would look even bleaker. The low visibility of Asian Americans in the U.S. political arena is intriguing and worth investigating.

According to Daniels (1988) and J. Wu and Song (2000), Asian Americans' political participation indeed lags far behind other racial minority groups. One possible explanation, according to Fong (1998) and Lien (1997), is that they are discouraged by past discriminations and other unsuccessful experiences in politics, which in turn intensifies Asian Americans' alienation from the democratic system. With a census figure less than 5% of the nation's population, no shared language or religious bond[2] among the widely diversified ethnicities, and vague geographic concentration of their residences, Asian Americans seemingly have had a bumpier road to reach the political arena than do other minorities. Lack of role models in politics also may have contributed to their disinterest and disengagement.

---

[1]An earlier version of this chapter appeared in the *Howard Journal of Communications, 16* (2005): 225–241.

[2]For example, unlike African or Latino Americans, Asian Americans might believe in Buddhism, Christianity, Hinduism, and Islam and speak more than 100 languages and dialects.

Mass media provide the most accessible and influential role models that audiences, especially children, can possibly imitate (e.g., Bandura, 1977; Wilson et al., 2002). Therefore, it is not surprising that media representations of racial, ethnic, and sexual minorities, as well as women, have been popular topics among communication scholars (e.g., Creedon, 1993; Entman & Rojecki, 2000; Gross, 2001; Kilbourne, 1999; Larson, 2006; Lester, 1996). However, research on news coverage of Asian Americans, especially Asian American politicians, has been scanty in comparison to other minority groups. This chapter attempts to bridge the gap by investigating newspaper coverage of five Asian American candidates who were involved in high-profile campaigns during 1993–2003.

CAMPAIGN COVERAGE

The news media are arguably the most important source of information for citizens to keep up with politics and make voting decisions (Graber, 2006; Joslyn, 1984; Neuman, Just, & Crigler, 1992). The news media often influence how people view political issues and candidates; therefore, directly or indirectly, they have powerful influence on public opinion and electoral results (Fallows, 1996; Glynn, Herbst, O'Keefe, Shapiro, & Lindeman, 2004; Graber, 2006; Johnson, Hays, & Hays, 1997; Wanta, 1997). Media impact on elections was well illustrated by Patterson (1980, 1994), who contended that what people see during an election is not the actual campaign, but the media's version of it. The media impact will be even stronger if the voters cannot otherwise evaluate the candidate, either via his track record in prior public service or his image as a public office holder. In the case of Asian American candidates who are rarely established in the political arena, their chance is more likely to be at the media's mercy.

Given the known tendency of media coverage, one would naturally suspect that campaign coverage of minority candidates would differ from that of mainstream candidates. It is worth examining whether a given group of candidates are more likely to receive negative or stereotypical coverage and, therefore, suffer from the disadvantage in races. As the following section of literature review indicates, empirical investigation on this line of inquiry is not satisfactory or sufficient: Only a few studies were done on the coverage of races in which African-American candidates were involved. The examinations of campaign coverage about other ethnicities are almost nonexistent. Some scholars (e.g., Citrin, Green, & Sears, 1990), however, argued that the gender and race of candidates does not necessarily have a significant impact on election outcomes.

What really matters, they contended, are candidates' track records, campaign style, and whether they are perceived by the electorate as "solid." Female candidates, for example, are often seen as less competent than their male counterparts, and thus they need to work harder to establish their credibility (Bernstein, 2000). Their image portrayed by the media is where they can start.

FACTORS BEHIND NEWS COVERAGE

Journalists and the institutions they work for usually are part of the mainstream culture. Mainstream ideologies and traditional values are often reflected in news coverage to appeal to the mass audience. Protest groups that hold anti-mainstream, avant-garde views, for example, are likely to receive marginalized or slanted coverage (Gitlin, 1980; Hallin, 1986; McLeod, 1995; McLeod & Detenber, 1999; Paletz & Entman, 1981). The daily decision of what news is and how to report it is, to a great extent, determined by the "enduring values" of society (Gans, 1979). Thus, to understand how Asian American candidates are covered in the news, one may need to examine the society's common attitudes toward this particular group.

The traditional image of Asian-Americans has been "inferior, threatening," but recently and occasionally has been described as "praiseworthy" (Kitano & Daniels, 2001). Once in a while, the term *model minority* would appear in the news to characterize the ethnic group's achievement and recognition in the society (Fong, 1998; Wong, 1994), which, to many Asian Americans, serves as a double-edged sword. As Takagi (1992) pointed out, many Asian Americans do not feel comfortable with the praise—usually bestowed by the conservatives, Asian Americans' unwanted ally—that can be used to downplay societal discrimination against Asian Americans and to justify their ineligibility for affirmative action.

Interestingly, despite the history and contribution that Asian Americans have made in U.S. society, they still are often seen by the majority of Americans as outsiders and certainly unlikely to be in power. As reported by Aoki and Nakanishi (2001), Congressman David Wu (D–Oregon), once was denied entrance to the U.S. Energy Department where he was invited to deliver a speech. Wu's congressional identification did not convince security guards that he was a U.S. citizen. A national survey (see Aoki & Nakanishi, 2001) indicated that half of the interviewed respondents doubt the loyalty of the Chinese American, suspecting they may pass secret information on to China.

Journalists, like average Americans, may harbor such similarly discriminatory attitudes toward Asian Americans but are not aware of them. Entman (1990) and Hemant and Thornton (1994) showed that careless and insensitive coverage of racial groups might actually promote racial stereotypes and resentments. The stereotype-saturated mindset in our society about Asian Americans may, one way or another, affect the way journalists report on Asian Americans and the issues in which they are involved. This is the logic behind the efforts to diversify the news personnel (Brislin & Williams, 1996; Craft & Wanta, 2003; Delaney, 1997; Zoch & Turk, 1998; also see chap. 4, this volume), which aims to elevating the capability of news media to cover the diversifying perspectives existing in our society.

This chapter (and the book) is timely considering the increasing number of Asian Americans and the sudden advance of several Asian American politicians on the national stage since the turn of the century. It is unprecedented that two cabinet members in the George W. Bush administration (Elaine Chao and Norman Mineta) were Asian American. Gary Locke became the first Asian American governor in U.S. history. However, political accusations of racial discrimination against Asian Americans still exist, such as the controversial arrest of nuclear scientist Wen Ho Lee and the illegal campaign contribution scandal during the Clinton administration ("Campaign Finance," 1998; R. Lee, 1999; Lee & Zia, 2002; Liu, 1998). The fundamental research question of the present exploratory inquiry is: How have selected Asian American candidates been covered by newspapers? Have the political candidates of this minority group been treated fairly by the press in comparison with other mainstream politicians? What are the attributes of the coverage, positive or negative, bestowed on the Asian American candidates?

MEDIA COVERAGE OF MINORITIES

Fair presence for minorities in the media seems to be the first criterion researchers use to examine content. Chaudhary (1980) and Barber and Gandy (1990) investigated press coverage of African-American public office holders and both found that African Americans actually received more stories than did their White counterparts. Based on the principle of proportional representation, Stevenson (1992), however, counted the number of ads with and without African-American models and suggested unfair treatment. In addition to sheer quantity of representation, how a minority group is actually portrayed is important because sometimes it is where the difference resides (Barber & Gandy, 1990). Studies concerned with this aspect inspected whether a racial or sexual minority is represented in the media in a stereotypical or negative way. A typical example can be found in Lester's (1996) *Images That Injure*, in which contributing authors analyze stereotypical visual coverage of women, African and Latin Americans, as well as gays and lesbians. Even in sports programming, racial stereotypes about professional athletes are often invoked. Rada (1996) found that White players are often described as intellectual, whereas African-American players are portrayed as purely athletic.

There is relatively little empirical, especially systematic and quantitative, research on media coverage or representation of Asians or Asian Americans. Lester's (1996) book, like many other similar scholarly efforts, examined only African, Latino, and Native Americans as well as Pacific Islanders (e.g., Hawaiians), yet entirely neglected Asian Americans. There are, however, studies that investigated the images of Asians or Asian Americans portrayed in TV dramas, movies, or popular cultures. For example, Gardner (1961) examined the roots of the Chinese images in U.S. history. Hamamoto (1994) traced the negative Asian images presented on American TV. Traditionally, according to Fong (1998), Asian roles in Hollywood movies are rare and, if present, tend to be stereotypical. For example, male characters tend to be asexual, cunning, but not very smart—Charlie Chan, Fu Manchu, and Jackie Chan may represent the category. Asian female characters, in contrast, tend to be exotic sex objects who are submissive or helpless and await heroes to come to their rescue. In a nutshell, these studies disclosed that Asians or/and Asian Americans trailed miserably in both volume and valence on mass media.

More recent anecdotal reports seem to confirm the aforementioned trends. Asian Americans are rarely seen on TV either in entertainment programs (Elber, 2000) or in newscast (Matsumoto, 1998; Sengupta, 1997). In rare occasions when roles were assigned to this group on TV and in movies, they are still mostly negative (Chao, 1998). Chen (1996) and Ni (1995) both observed that Asian men are often portrayed either sexless or feminized. Asian women, in contrast, are still confined to traditional and stereotypical roles (Braxton, 1999).

The studies reviewed previously mainly focus on representation of the Asian American in entertainment media. One cannot help but wonder whether the Asian American political aspirants have received similar treatment in the news. Specifically, did the five Asian American political candidates analyzed in this chapter receive equal treatment in the news as their non-Asian counterparts? To approach this question better, two other areas of literature need to be reviewed.

MEDIA COVERAGE OF MINORITY CANDIDATES

The majority of the studies that examined media coverage of minority candidates focused on African-American candidates. Zilber and Niven (2000), for example, analyzed the news coverage of African-American members of the Congress and found that the media devoted equally to covering all candidates and that they are more likely to mention the race of African-American candidates while typically ignoring the race or ethnicity of White candidates. This observation is echoed by Terkildsen and Damore (1999), who also looked at the coverage of congressional candidates. Additionally, Zilber and Niven (2000) indicated that the news discusses racial issues much more when African-American candidates are involved. In line with this, when covering African-American candidates, the media emphasized the racial composition of the district and partisan orientation (Terkildsen & Damore, 1999).

Although local elections are more likely to result in the election of minority candidates because they are feasible to muster sufficient votes from the candidate's ethnic group, it is still important for minority candidates to reach out to other ethnic groups. The media's aforementioned tendency of covering statewide elections also was found in case studies that looked at local elections. Sylvie's (1995) examination of a mayoral race concludes that Black candidates received more stories on ethical qualities than on their issue stances. A survey of media coverage of political races involving gays, lesbians, bisexual, and transgender candidates shows that the media appear to follow a similar mode of treating African-American candidates by characterizing them as "gay candidates," leaving out the candidates' platforms and key issues (George, 2002). One slight difference between African-American and gay candidates is that the latter group overall seems to receive a more positive tone in coverage. Looking at coverage across gender lines, Kahn (1994) found that female candidates tend to be treated less favorably by the press. The media devote more time to covering the viability of women candidates rather than their stances on key issues. Additionally, reporters are "less responsive to the issue and trait agendas of women candidates when compared to their male colleagues" (Kahn & Gordon, 1997, p. 73). So far, the existing literature has yet provided solid, comprehensive evidence as to what kind of news coverage Asian American candidates tend to receive during campaign periods.

FAIRNESS, BALANCE, AND GENERAL QUALITY

Objectivity is a tenet that mainstream journalists embrace, and a key element in commonly held journalistic ethics. Essentially, it means being neutral, unbiased, detached, and nonpartisan, and it can be translated to "accuracy, balance and fairness" in reporting (Achenbach, 1991; Merrill, 1997; Mindich, 1998; Reese, 1990; Streckfuss, 1990). Accuracy, although easy to understand, is more difficult to achieve and measure. It also is hard to quantify. Balance and fairness, however, can be operationalized as equal amounts of coverage given to all sides of an issue or all the candidates in a race. To examine fairness of news stories, researchers take into account the number of relevant news articles, length and location of each article, as well as the tone (favorability, neutrality, or negativity) in describing either side (Blumberg, 1954; Clarke & Evans, 1983; Fico, Ku, & Soffin, 1994; Kirman, 1992; Simon, Fico, & Lacy, 1989; Stempel & Windhauser, 1984). Quantity and placement of stories in relation to fairness are self-explanatory and can easily be operated in content coding. Regarding the qualitative aspects of campaign coverage, the media have been found focusing on game plans, strategies and tactics, or the "horse race," rather than on the substance (Graber, 2006; Joslyn, 1984; Lichter, Amundson, & Noyes, 1988). Also, media seem to pay ample attention to candidates' images, and personal characters or private lives, rather than public office seekers' issue stances (Sabato, 1991, 1994; Stempel & Windhauser, 1991). The present study endeavors to incorporate all of the aforementioned elements.

RESEARCH QUESTIONS

Given the findings of surveyed literature and the fact that mainstream journalists may not have much experience covering Asian American candidates in political races, it would be highly interesting to see whether the campaign coverage is steeped in stereotypes about Asian Americans and deviates from the traditional tenets of objective journalism. Accordingly, we developed the following explorative research questions:

RQ1. Did the news coverage of the election campaigns involving Asian American candidates demonstrate fairness and balance?

RQ1a. Did the Asian American candidates receive the same amount of coverage as their opponents?

RQ1b. Did the Asian American candidates receive the same level of valence in the news stories as their opponents?

RQ2. Were the Asian American candidates' racial or ethnic backgrounds mentioned more often or in more detail than their opponents?

RQ3. Were the Asian American candidates portrayed as "fringe" or mainstream candidates?

RQ4. Did the coverage of the Asian American candidates reveal any positive or negative racial stereotypes or images?

METHOD

Content analysis was used to record the elements of news stories that covered the five races that involved Asian American candidates. The fundamental attributes of news stories, such as dateline, bylines, and number of paragraphs, were included in the coding scheme. To successfully answer the research questions, coders evaluated each story's overall valence and recorded images and stereotypes associated with Asian American candidates. For example, the coding sheet asks the coder to check whether the "model minority" expression was invoked in the story, whether the candidate was described as good at math and science, and whether such adjectives as *submissive* or *indecisive* were used to describe the candidate. The coding sheet also includes 14 items that aim to record varied mentions of voter supports—White or minority—to unveil the portrayal of "fringe" or mainstream status of the Asian American candidates. For example, one of the coding items asks whether the story states that the candidate will receive support from White voters, whereas another one asks whether the story depicts the candidate in the story only representing the interest of minorities.

Additionally, coders identified news topics and frames employed by reporters. The researchers adopted Hofstetter's (1978) operationalization of favorable and unfavorable coverage of political candidates. According to Hofstetter, favorable coverage would contain the following elements: winning or gaining; being successful, skilled, a hard worker, diligent, or responsible; being greeted by a favorable crowd reaction or approval. Unfavorable attributes of a candidate would include: losing, losing support or failing; being negligent, lazy, foolish, and irresponsible; and being greeted by an unfavorable crowd reaction or disapproval. Coders were required to evaluate the overall tone for each candidate after reading a story. If the description cannot be classified as predominantly favorable or unfavorable for either candidate, then it was coded as mixed or neutral.

The campaigns analyzed in this chapter include five high-profile races that took place on the West Coast and the South during 1993–2003: the mayoral election of Los Angeles in 1993 (Michael Woo vs. Richard

Riordan), the gubernatorial election in Washington in 1996 (Gary Locke vs. Ellen Craswell), the congressional race in the first district (Portland) of Oregon in 1998 (David Wu vs. Molly Bordonaro), the U.S. senatorial race between Matt Fong and Barbara Boxer in 1998 (California), and the gubernatorial race of Louisiana in 2003 (Bobby Jindal vs. Kathleen Blanco). These five races were selected because no incumbents were involved in them—thus, no candidate was in an advantageous position. Also, the electorates in the races were diverse enough that the Asian American candidates needed votes outside their ethnic constituencies. Each of the races involved an Asian American candidate and a Euro-American opponent. Three of the Asian American candidates (Locke, Wu, and Woo) are Democrats and their opponents Republicans. The results of these three races, however, are slightly different—the former two races ended in electing the Asian American candidates (Locke and Wu), whereas the race of the Los Angeles mayor did not. Both Asian American GOP tickets (Fong and Jindal) included in this study lost to their Democratic opponents. The authors hoped that by including both successful and unsuccessful Asian American candidates for various offices, the investigation might result in a more comprehensive finding.

The newspaper articles were collected either from Lexis/Nexis or from the CD-ROM of a newspaper's archive using key words (candidates' names) to search every relevant story. As long as the names of either candidate in each race appear in the body of the news, the story was included in our sample. The Seattle *Times* was selected to represent the coverage of the Washington state gubernatorial race, the *Oregonian* was used for the coverage of the congressional race of the first district of Oregon, the San Francisco *Chronicle* was chosen for the Fong–Boxer race, the coverage of both the New Orleans *Times-Picayune* and the Baton Rouge *Advocate* was studied for the 2003 Louisiana gubernatorial race, and the Los Angeles *Times* was examined for its coverage of the mayoral race in 1993. Except for the San Francisco *Chronicle* and the Baton Rouge *Advocate*, the papers examined in the study have the biggest circulation in the four states, respectively. The decision to opt for the *Chronicle*—rather than the LA *Times*—for the 1998 California senatorial campaign and the inclusion of the Baton Rouge *Advocate* (in addition to the New Orleans paper, which did not cover as much as others) was based purely on the idea of broadening our sample of newspapers. The study period for each race is 1 year—an entire year's coverage about each race prior to the election day was included.

After excluding such non-news items as letters to the editors and one-line appearance announcements, 898 news stories were selected for our analysis. Specifically, 210 stories were from the LA *Times* in 1993

(23.4%), 138 stories from the Seattle *Times* in 1996 (15.4%), 87 stories from the *Times-Picayune* (9.7%), 211 stories from the *Advocate* (23.5%), 146 stories from the SF *Chronicle* (16.3%), and 106 stories from the *Oregonian* in 1998 (11.8%). Two trained coders performed the coding: One is an African-American female in her early 20s, and the other is an Asian American male in his 30s. Both are familiar with U.S. politics and have a substantial knowledge of mass communication. Intercoder reliability was calculated based on their coding of 20 news stories, and the average alpha for the coding items is 93% using Holsti's formula.[3]

FINDINGS

Of the six papers examined, the LA *Times* and the Baton Rouge *Advocate* had published more stories on their respective campaign than did the other four papers—the San Francisco *Chronicle* (146), the Seattle *Times* (138), the *Oregonian* (106), and the New Orleans *Times-Picayune* (87). Most of the news stories were reported by the six papers' staff writers (89%), and most of the identifiable reporters are males (72%).

Regarding the primary focus of the election stories, as expected, most of them are about the horse race (58.3%), and only one in four stories is about issue and policy (24.6%) (see Table 3.1). Of the stories that mention the Asian American candidates, 65.9% discuss horse race between the candidates, followed by issue and policy (35.0%), image of the candidate (18.4%), and candidate's qualifications (10.1%). The Euro-American candidates seem to have attracted a similar pattern of new coverage. The only major difference resides in the horse-race topic—the Euro-American candidates did not receive as much on the topic as did the Asian American counterparts. Perhaps reporters were more interested in reporting the odds of the unusual—Asian American—candidates winning the offices.

---

[3]The two coders agreed 1,269 out of 1,630 times, excluding "mechanical" items such as titles, dates, and page numbers. The following is the breakdown of agreements among coding categories: (a) number of total paragraphs (100%); (b) number of paragraphs devoted to each candidate (85%); (c) identification of candidates and opponents in articles (85%); (d) favorability (63%); (e) number of paragraphs about candidates' racial/ethnic background (90%); (f) number of paragraphs about candidates' support or nonsupport from racial minorities and majorities (88.8%); (g) racial stereotypes about Asian American candidates (98.6%); (h) description of Asian American candidates (98.8%); (i) description of opponent candidates (99.4%); and (j) types of coverage (84.7%).

Table 3.1
News Topics by Candidates*

Primary Topic	Asian American		Euro-American		Overall Story	
	%	n	%	n	%	n
Horse race	65.9	592	59.4	533	58.3	522
Issue and policy	35.0	314	36.1	324	24.6	220
Image	18.4	165	17.8	160	4.7	42
Qualification	10.1	91	10.2	92	2.5	22
Other/mixed	15.0	135	21.5	193	9.9	89

*N = 898. Total of column percentage may exceed 100 due to multiple answers.

Fairness and Balance

There are 18,842 paragraphs in the 898 stories from the six papers. Therefore, on average, a story has about 21 paragraphs. The five Asian American candidates were included in 5,817 paragraphs, whereas their opponents were mentioned in 5,693 paragraphs—both the Asian Americans and their opponents gained roughly 6.5 paragraphs in a given story, indicating the Asian American candidates and their opponents received, on average, approximately equal amount of coverage (t = .354, df = 5, p = .738). Yet when one compares the volumes across the papers (see Table 3.2), interestingly only the two California papers gave slightly less newshole to the two Asian American candidates (Fong and Woo), who coincidentally lost their races to the Euro-American opponents (Boxer and Riordan).

Table 3.2
Paragraphs by Candidates in Each Paper

Paper	Asian American (n)	Euro-American (n)
LA *Times*	1,693	1,876
Portland *Oregonian*	622	558
Seattle *Times*	867	761
New Orleans *Times-Picayune*	425	382
Baton Rouge *Advocate*	1,278	1,073
San Francisco *Chronicle*	932	1,043

Note. Asian American (M = 969.6) vs. White (M = 948.8).
t = .354, df = 5, p = .738.

As for favorability, we evaluated each story that mentioned either candidate with a three-category scale: positive, neutral/mixed, and negative. The mean score of overall favorability for the Asian American candidates in the stories is 2.13 (based on 749 coded stories; $SD = .97$), and their counterparts have received an average of 2.10 (based on 700 coded stories; $SD = .64$). It appears that the Asian American candidates were covered slightly more positively, although the difference is statistically insignificant ($t = .87$, $df = 1,447$, $p = .387$), and their coverage's valence fluctuates more than that of the White counterparts. With the evidence about volume and valence of the news coverage between the five Asian American candidates and their opponents, we conclude that the coverage overall is fair and balanced.

Ethnic Backgrounds

A total of 151 paragraphs in the studied news stories identified Asian American candidates' racial or ethnic backgrounds. In contrast, their opponents' racial or ethnic backgrounds were mentioned in only 28 paragraphs. A statistical test was performed, and the difference between ethnic mentions turned out statistically significant ($t = 5.06$, $df = 1,789$, $p < .001$), indicating Asian American candidates' ethnic backgrounds appeared more often in the news stories than did the equivalent information of their Euro-American counterparts. It is interesting that the general term *Asian American* was rarely used in the articles to describe the Asian American candidates; such ethnicity-specific terms as *Chinese American* or *Indian American* were more commonly used. Although *White* or *Caucasian* were used to identify Bordonaro, Craswell, or Riordan, specific terms like *Italian American* or *German American* were not invoked in the news stories, nor did the stories introduce the ethnic background of any of the five Euro-American candidates. The only exceptions were Richard Riordan, who was identified as Irish American twice by the *LA Times*, and Barbara Boxer, who was identified as Jewish once by the *SF Chronicle*. This striking difference can be extrapolated that Asian American candidates are still a novelty to average American voters and, therefore, their unusual background is newsworthy.

Fringe or Mainstream Candidates

Any Asian American public office seeker cannot be elected by Asian American voters alone; they need to appear mainstream and reach out to other ethnic groups. Sometimes news coverage of ethnic-based voting for a given candidate can serve as a telling signal to the electorate and further demarcate the constituencies across the ethnic line, resulting in a fringe image of the minority candidate. A total of 179 paragraphs in the six papers stated that Asian American candidates are supported by racial minorities, whereas only 61 paragraphs indicated such a tendency for their Euro-American opponents. The difference is statistically significant ($t = 4.20$, $df = 1,792$, $p < .001$).

By comparison, 29 paragraphs indicated that the White candidates in the five races are likely to be supported by the racial majority, whereas only in 15 paragraphs did the stories report the Asian American candidates gain the supports from Whites. However, the difference of White supports between the two groups of candidates is statistically insignificant ($t = -1.58$, $df = 1,792$, $p = .115$), which could be attributed to the fact that the majority of the stories did not mention this sort of relation. Additionally, 18 paragraphs mentioned that the Asian American candidates are opposed by White voters, whereas nowhere in the stories could we find the same indication of tendency toward the Euro-American candidates.

Significant differences also were found between the two groups of candidates in terms of racially related descriptions used in the stories. First of all, the Asian American candidates were described to receive support from mostly racial minorities in the races in 44 stories, whereas in 23 stories the White candidates were said to receive support from mostly White constituents. In addition, seven news stories predicted that if the Asian American candidate got elected, the candidate would only represent the interests of racial minorities, but not the general constituency. In contrast, White candidates were described in eight stories that, if elected, they would represent not only the interest of minorities. Despite the low frequency, the stories appeared to provide a divisive picture along the race line. However, the Asian American candidates or their ancestors were more likely than their White opponents to be described to embody the American dream (31 mentions). This could be perceived as a positive descriptor, yet could imply the candidate's new immigrant background or even be interpreted as patronizing in tone. Interestingly, Asian American candidates sometimes play this theme in the press to their advantage. For example, in his publicized resignation letter to President George W. Bush in the beginning of his campaign, Jindal said, "I now leave your great administration to consider an exciting leadership opportunity in my home state of Louisiana, and to further pursue the American Dream" (Walsh, 2003, p. 2). Both Locke and Wu campaigns also highlighted the theme of the American dream.

Although the frequency of describing Asian American candidates only supported by minorities is not high and the instances of mentioning opposition from White voters toward the Asian American candidates in the stories are not abundant, most differences between the news coverage about the Asian American candidates and their counterparts are statistically significant. Therefore, we argue that, despite the low frequency of fringe attributes associated with the Asian American candidates, the distinctive news treatments of the two groups of candidates are still worth stressing.

Stereotypes

The two attributes about the Asian American candidates that appeared most frequently in the news stories are "submissive, indecisive, or shy" (62 times) and "cunning, calculated, and prone to corruption" (46 times)—both are utterly negative for politicians. The third on the list of most frequent stereotypes, however, could arguably be a positive one: "model minority" (overachieving, aggressive, striving to succeed) (30 times). Another negative attribute for the Asian American candidates is stingy and/or greedy, which appeared 16 times in the news stories examined.

Other adjectives that were used to depict the Asian American candidates are: traditional (eight times); thin, short, or physically weak (five times); good at math and sciences (three times); and like to associate with own kind (two times). Another enduring misperception about Asians in the nation is that they are likely to be foreigners. This perspective is echoed in the occasional mentions of the Asian American candidates' source of campaign funding that might be illegal and could come from foreign nationals or foreign agents. In several stories, the reporters, assuming the candidate's connection with Asian countries, wrote that the candidate's ethnic background might be beneficial to global business and international relations with Asia. It appears that the pictures of the Asian American candidates the reporters portrayed are in sync with the images that the entertainment media have been providing.

DISCUSSION

This chapter sets out to study the election coverage of five races in distinct West Coast and Southern states where Whites constitute the majority of the population and any office holder would have to collect the support from constituents that belong to other races and ethnicities. Based on the findings presented, we conclude that the Asian American candidates seemingly have received a similar amount of news coverage as their Euro-American opponents in the five elections between 1993 and 2003. The output from the news coding also suggests that overall the news coverage is fair and balanced across the campaign camps. Regarding the topics of the coverage, we found that there exists only minor discrepancy of coverage between the Asian American and the Euro-American candidates—most of the stories focused on the horse race, and only about two fifths of the news stories pertained to candidates' issue stances and public policies.

The authors, however, cannot draw the conclusion that the news coverage is completely free of flaws. It is found that some undertones and subjective, loaded adjectives might have distinguished the news coverage between the Asian American and the Euro-American candidates. Despite the low frequency of stereotypes embedded in the news stories, we believe their appearances may stick out from the ordinary text to grasp readers' attention, thus forming an instant negative framing effect. Some of the clichéd descriptions about the Asian American candidates can invoke or strengthen readers' existing bias. A substantial number of the stories described the Asian American candidates as submissive, indecisive, and shy; others attached such adjectives as cunning, calculated, and inscrutable with the Asian American candidates, echoing those repugnant fictional characters such as Charlie Chan in some Hollywood-made films. Although a couple of overachieving, arguably positive images were used sometimes in the stories—such as "model minority" and the American dream embodied in the candidate, the overall picture provided for the Asian American candidates is not flattering.

Although two of the five examined races resulted in sending Asian American candidates to the offices, it does not necessarily mean that the slanted coverage did not damage the Asian American candidates. For one thing, their campaigns could have been more successful in capturing more votes if the news stories had used a more positive tone. Gary Locke's campaign strategist, Blair Butterworth, and David Wu told us in phone interviews that their opponents' extremely conservative stands on various issues—versus Locke's middle-of-the-road approach—helped tremendously. Thus, election results simply cannot justify the way the Asian American candidates were portrayed and the races were covered in the press.

Given that roughly 10% of the West Coast population are Asian descendants (comparatively high in the lower 48 states) and that Asian Americans have been living in this region for probably more than one and half centuries, one would expect that journalists of this region know better about Asian Americans and readers would demand more sensitive coverage. The finding about the recurring usage of stereotypical adjectives in the news stories for the Asian American candidates is worth pondering. One may wonder what kind of coverage Gary Locke would have received had he run in another region of the nation that has a smaller Asian American population, such as the deep South. This is where the Jindal campaign comes in. This uncommon election has helped us shed some light on the scenario where the majority of the electorate is unfamiliar with the heritage of the candidate. Despite the fair coverage even found in the Louisiana papers, it is still too early for researchers to assert that the barrier for Asian American political candidates to receive completely fair, unbiased coverage has been brushed away. Although utterly prejudiced coverage seems to disappear in the news, subtly disapproving and disadvantageous coverage may still linger. Aspiring Asian American politicians need to cope with this challenge, whereas political journalists need to address and work on this aspect of problem in covering campaigns.

This study certainly has limitations that should be addressed. For one thing, the sample of Asian American candidates under investigation would have been more representative if women candidates were included in the study. Unfortunately, no Asian female candidates had run campaigns at this level. Asian Americans are known to be vitally diversified in politics—it is even challenging for political pundits to predict the relationship between an Asian ethnicity and its political party affiliation. Therefore, including more diversifying cases should be emphasized for future investigations. Second, all of the candidates included in this study are nonincumbents. It would be intriguing to see whether news coverage about Asian American incumbents are portrayed differently and whether the often-associated adjectives, such as *indecisive* and *submissive*, still appear in the news. Last, this chapter only included newspaper as the study sample. Given the known influence of TV and the ever-popular Internet, the audiovideo parts of campaign coverage should not be neglected in future endeavors. This study is only a modest attempt, and hopefully more of this kind of content investigation will follow.

REFERENCES

Achenbach, J. (1991, November/December). Oh, that code of ethics, *The Quill*, pp. 22–23.

Aoki, A. L., & Nakanishi, D. T. (2001, September 3). Asian Pacific Americans and the new minority politics. *PS: Political Science & Politics, 34*, 605–610.

Bandura, A. (1977). *Social learning theory*. Englewood Cliffs, NJ: Prentice-Hall.

Barber, J. T., & Gandy, O. H., Jr. (1990). Press portrayal of African American and white United States Representatives. *The Howard Journal of Communications, 2*(2), 213–225.

Bernstein, A. G. (2000). The effects of message theme, policy explicitness, and candidate gender. *Communication Quarterly, 48*(2), 159–173.

Blumberg, N. B. (1954). *One-party press? Coverage of the 1952 presidential campaign in 35 daily newspapers.* Lincoln: University of Nebraska Press.

Braxton, G. (1999, July 24). Faced with reality of exclusion, minority writers, actors say emphasis on young whites has put their livelihood at risk. *The Los Angeles Times,* p. 1.

Brislin, T., & Williams, N. (1996). Beyond diversity: Expanding the canon in journalism ethics. *Journal of Mass Media Ethics, 11*(1), 16–27.

Campaign Finance Key Player: John Huang. (1998). Retrieved October 17, 2003, from http://www.washingtonpost.com/wp-srv/politics/special/campfin/players/huang.htm

Chao, J. (1998, September 9). Asian Americans gaining more roles, but still often cast in negative light. *The Seattle Post-Intelligencer,* p. D3.

Chaudhary, A. G. (1980). Press portrayal of black officials. *Journalism Quarterly, 57,* 636–641.

Chen, C. H. (1996). Feminization of Asian (American) men in the U.S. mass media: An analysis of the Ballad of Little Jo. *Journal of Communication Inquiry, 20*(2), 57–71.

Citrin, J., Green, D. P., & Sears, D. O. (1990). White reactions to black candidates: When does race matter? *Public Opinion Quarterly, 54*(1), 74–96.

Clarke, P., & Evans, S. H. (1983). *Covering campaigns: Journalism in congressional elections.* Stanford, CA: Stanford University Press.

Craft, S., & Wanta, W. (2003). Women in the newsroom: Influences of female editors and reporters on the news agenda. *Journalism & Mass Communication Quarterly, 81,* 1.

Creedon, P. J. (Ed.). (1993). *Women in mass communication* (2nd ed.). Newbury Park, CA: Sage.

Daniels, R. (1988). *Asian American: Chinese and Japanese in the United States since 1850.* Seattle: University of Washington Press.

Delaney, P. (1997). The black vanguard integrates newsrooms. *Media Studies Journal, 11*(2), 17–21.

Elber, L. (2000, November 16). Diversity on TV still lacking, group say. *The Columbian* (Vancouver, WA), p. A7.

Entman, R. M. (1990). Modern racism and the images of blacks in local television news. *Critical Studies in Mass Communication, 7*(4), 332–345.

Entman, R. M., & Rojecki, A. (2000). *The black image in the white mind: Media and race in America.* Chicago: University of Chicago Press.

Fallows, J. (1996). *Breaking the news: How the media undermine American democracy.* New York: Pantheon.

Fico, F., Ku, L., & Soffin, S. (1994). Fairness, balance of newspaper coverage of U.S. in Gulf War. *Newspaper Research Journal, 15,* 30–43.

Fong, T. P. (1998). *The contemporary Asian American experience: Beyond the model minority.* Upper Saddle River, NJ: Prentice-Hall.

Gans, H. J. (1979). *Deciding what's news.* New York: Vintage Books.

Gardner, J. G. (1961). *The image of the Chinese in the United States, 1885–1915.* Unpublished doctoral dissertation in American Civilization, University of Pennsylvania, Philadelphia, PA.

George, M. (2002). *Case study of media coverage of gay candidates.* Unpublished manuscript from the University of Southern California, Annenberg School for Communication, Los Angeles, CA.

Gitlin, T. (1980). *The whole world is watching: News media in the making and unmaking of the new left.* Berkeley, CA: University of California Press.

Glynn, C. J., Herbst, S., O'Keefe, G. J., Shapiro, R. Y., & Lindeman, M. (2004). *Public opinion.* Boulder, CO: Westview.

Graber, D. A. (2006). *Mass media and American politics.* Washington, DC: CQ Press.

Greenfield, J. (1982). *The real campaign: How the media missed the story of the 1980 campaign.* New York: Summit Books.

Gross, L. (2001). *Up from invisibility: Lesbians, gay men, and the media in America.* New York: Columbia University Press.

Hallin, D. C. (1986). *The "uncensored war": The media and Vietnam.* New York: Oxford University Press.

Hamamoto, D. Y. (1994). *Monitored peril: Asian Americans and the politics of TV representation.* Minneapolis: University of Minnesota Press.

Hemant, S., & Thornton, M. C. (1994). Racial ideology in the U.S. mainstream news magazine coverage of Black-Latino interaction, 1980–1992. *Critical Studies in Mass Communication, 11*(2), 141–161.

Hofstetter, R. C. (1978, November). News bias in the 1972 campaign: A cross-media comparison. *Journalism Monographs, 58.*

Johnson, T. J., Hays, C. E., & Hays, S. P. (Eds.). (1997). *Engaging the public: How government and the media can reinvigorate American democracy.* New York: Rowman & Littlefield.

Joslyn, R. (1984). *Mass media elections.* Reading, MA: Addison-Wesley.

Kahn, K. F. (1994). The distorted mirror: Press coverage of women candidates for statewide office. *Journal of Politics, 56*(1), 154–174.

Kahn, K. F., & Gordon, A. (1997). How women campaign for the U.S. Senate: Substance and strategy. In P. Norris (Ed.), *Women, media and politics* (pp. 59–76). New York: Oxford University Press.

Kilbourne, J. (1999). *Deadly persuasion: Why women and girls must fight the addictive power of advertising.* New York: The Free Press.

Kirman, J. M. (1992). Using newspapers to study media bias. *Social Education,* 47–51.

Kitano, H. H. L., & Daniels, R. (2001). *Asian Americans: Emerging minorities* (3rd ed.). Upper Saddle River, NJ: Prentice-Hall.

Larson, S. G. (2006). *Media & minorities: The politics of race in news and entertainment.* Lanham, MD: Rowman & Littlefield.

Lee, W. H., & Zia, H. (2002). *My country versus me: The first-hand account by the Los Alamos scientist who was falsely accused of being a spy.* New York: Hyperion.

Lester, P. M. (Ed.). (1996). *Images that injure: Pictorial stereotypes in the media.* Westport, CT: Praeger.

Lichter, S. R., Amundson, D., & Noyes, R. (1988). *The video campaign: Network coverage of the 1988 primaries.* Washington, DC: American Enterprise Institute for Public Policy Research.

Lien, P. (1997). *The political participation of Asian Americans: Voting behavior in Southern California.* New York: Garland.

Liu, E. (1998). *The accidental Asian: Notes of a native speaker.* New York: Random House.

Matsumoto, J. (1998, September 4). Asian Americans anchor their influence: Television. *The Los Angeles Times,* p. 2.

McLeod, D. M. (1995). Communicating deviance: The effects of television news coverage of social protest. *Journal of Broadcasting and Electronic Media, 39*(1), 4–19.

McLeod, D. M., & Detenber, B. H. (1999). Framing effects of television news coverage of social protest. *Journal of Communication, 49*(3), 3–23.

Merrill, J. C. (1997). *Journalism ethics: Philosophical foundations for news media.* New York: St. Martin's Press.

Mindich, D. T. Z. (1998). *Just the facts: How "objectivity" came to define American journalism.* New York: New York University Press.

Neuman, W. R., Just, M. R., & Crigler, A. N. (1992). *Common knowledge: News and construction of political meaning.* Chicago: University of Chicago Press.

Ni, C. (1995, February 23). Shedding their shirts—and a stereotype entrepreneurship: Sexless computer nerds? *The Los Angeles Times,* p. 1.

Paletz, D. L., & Entman, R. M. (1981). *Media power politics.* New York: The Free Press.

Patterson, T. E. (1980). *The mass media election: How Americans choose their president.* New York: Praeger.

Patterson, T. E. (1994). *Out of order.* New York: Vintage Books.

Rada, J. A. (1996). Color blind-sided: Racial bias in network television's coverage of professional football games. *The Howard Journal of Communications, 7*(3), 231–239.

Reese, S. D. (1990). The news paradigm and the ideology of objectivity: A socialist at the *Wall Street Journal. Critical Studies in Mass Communication, 7,* 390–409.

Sabato, L. J. (1991). *Feeding frenzy: How attack journalism has transformed American politics.* New York: The Free Press.

Sabato, L. J. (1994). Open season: How the news media cover presidential campaigns in the age of attack journalism. In D. A. Graber (Ed.), *Media power in politics* (pp. 193–203). Washington, DC: CQ Press.

Sengupta, S. (1997, Winter–Spring). The Connie Chung phenomenon. *Media Studies Journal, 7*(1 & 2), 183–196.

Simon, T., Fico, F., & Lacy, S. (1989). Covering conflict and controversy: Measuring balance, fairness, defamation. *Journalism Quarterly, 66,* 427–434.

Stempel, G. H. III, & Windhauser, J. W. (1984). The prestige press revisited: Coverage of the 1980 presidential campaign. *Journalism Quarterly, 61,* 49–55.

Stempel, G. H. III, & Windhauser, J. W. (Eds.). (1991). *The media in the 1984 and 1988 presidential campaigns.* New York: Greenwood.

Stevenson, T. H. (1992). A content analysis of the portrayals of Blacks in trade publication advertising. *Journal of Current Issues and Research in Advertising, 14*, 67–74.

Streckfuss, R. (1990). Objectivity in journalism: A search and a reassessment. *Journalism Quarterly, 67*, 973–983.

Sylvie, G. (1995). Black mayoral candidates and the press: Running for coverage. *The Howard Journal of Communications, 6*(1 & 2), 89–101.

Takagi, D. Y. (1992). *The retreat from race: Asian American admissions and racial politics.* New Brunswick, NJ: Rutgers University Press.

Terkildsen, N., & Damore, D. F. (1999). The dynamics of racialized media coverage in congressional elections. *The Journal of Politics, 61*(3), 680–699.

Walsh, B. (2003, February 14). Ex-Foster aide resigns post as Bush health-care adviser; Gubernatorial bid possibly in the works. *Times-Picayune*, national, p. 2.

Wanta, W. (1997). *How people learn about important issues: The public and the national agenda.* Mahwah, NJ: Erlbaum.

Wilson, B. J., Smith, S. L., Potter, W. J., Kunkel, D., Linz, D., Colvin, C. M., & Donnerstein, E. (2002). Violence in children's television programming: Assessing the risks. *Journal of Communication, 52*(1), 5–35.

Wong, W. (1994). Covering the invisible "model minority." *Media Studies Journal, 8*(3), 49–59.

Wu, J. Y. S., & Song, M. (Eds.). (2000). *Asian American studies: A reader.* New Brunswick, NJ: Rutgers University Press.

Zilber, J., & Niven, D. (2000). Congress and the news media: Stereotypes in the news media coverage of African-Americans in Congress. *Harvard International Journal of Press/Politics, 5*(1), 32–49.

Zoch, L. M., & Turk, J. V. (1998). Women making news: Gender as a variable in source selection and use. *Journalism & Mass Communication Quarterly, 75*(4), 762–775.

Chapter 4

Relationships Between Asian American Staff and Asian American Coverage in U.S. Newspapers[1]

H. Denis Wu and Ralph Izard

Conventional wisdom holds that the number of reporters from an ethnic group in the newsroom is highly relevant to the quantity as well as quality of the newspaper's coverage about the ethnic group. Advocates (Adams & Cleary, 2006) argued that the ethnic background of a reporter/editor is crucial to his or her understanding and coverage of issues and incidents related to a given ethnic group. This is the rationale of the American Society of Newspaper Editors (ASNE), an organization that has pushed for years to add minority staffs into newsrooms (American Society of Newspaper Editors, 1999). Nevertheless, little solid evidence exists to support this widely upheld idea.

The fact that no empirical evidence exists to support the idea that more minority newsroom staffing improves quality and quantity of total community coverage is embarrassing to journalism organizations. Associations of minority journalists (e.g., Asian American Journalists Association [AAJA], National Association of Hispanic Journalists [NAHJ], and National Association of Black Journalists [NABJ]) and other professional, civic, and ethnic organizations have been lobbying media firms to hire and retain more ethnically diverse news professionals. The idea is that this will strengthen the breadth of newsroom perspective, broaden

[1]Another version of this research report appeared in the *Journalism and Mass Communication Quarterly*, 2008.

coverage of a community, and improve coverage of the nation's ethnic groups. Also, it is a good business practice because American people are more diverse than ever, and they would like to have their views reflected in their community newspapers.

This research project aimed to focus on Asian Americans as a case study and investigated whether the presence of Asian American journalists in the newsroom might have contributed to elevated quantity and quality of news stories related to Asian Americans. We also were interested in knowing whether their presence might have influenced news topics that pertain to Asian Americans. Additionally, we asked whether the stories done by Asian American journalists would score higher in the attribute assessments, including explanation, substance, perspective diversity, and, finally, contextual information.

REVIEW OF LITERATURE

For many years, mass communication researchers and working journalists have contributed to a national discussion of the value of diversity to the news media. Further, one finds general agreement that news organizations have failed in their efforts to achieve what generally is called parity—that is, developing staffs that represent the communities they seek to serve.

That many in the industry have good intentions is beyond dispute, and many have devoted considerable attention and efforts to increase their minority staff representation. These have resulted in some examples of excellence, but, in general, the record has not been encouraging (e.g., Knight Foundation report; Dedman & Doig, 2005). ASNE has set a goal of newspapers reaching minority parity, which it believes will be 38.2% representation—by 2025 (American Society of Newspaper Editors, 1999). Establishment of this goal follows an initial effort that was aborted in 1998 because of industry failure to achieve parity staffing by 2000. ASNE's (2005) annual newsroom census determined that newspaper minority staffing in 2004 stood at 13.4%, compared with a 31.7% national minority population level.

Arguments about the value of staff diversity have taken many forms—moral, cultural, and economic—and research likewise has been extensive and varied. Most recently, the need has been highlighted by projections that indicate minorities collectively will exceed half of the population by 2050 (U.S. Census Bureau, 2006). Taking note of this prediction, diversity proponents have intensified their arguments that the need is great for the media to make additional staffing efforts to ensure their coverage of the total communities they serve.

For example, Adams and Cleary (2006) point explicitly to the need for a broadening of coverage attitude by the total staffs of news organizations, including both the reporters and their leadership. "It follows," they say, "that if the staff setting the mores in a newsroom are not attuned to minority concerns, those standards will reflect that lack of sensitivity and the staff will receive the message that those concerns are not a priority with the editors" (p. 48). It also stands to reason that message will be perceived by media audiences.

It is not just scholars who see the problem. Clearly, although its past efforts have met minimal success, ASNE has maintained diversity as a subject of intense interest. Other professional organizations, such as the Society of Professional Journalists, the Radio-Television News Directors Association, and, of course, those representing minority journalists, have joined the effort. Much has been written on the subject. Shipler (1998), for example, quotes a White reporter for the Baltimore *Sun*: "Any white journalist in a town that's predominantly black begins to feel like it's more and more of a problem. It's a practical problem in the sense that you literally don't find out about stories. . . ." Shipler also notes the "public relations problems" created in the community as a result of inadequate diversity in staffing and coverage.

The problem is not simply a matter of numbers. The broadest fear is of the impact of the media on their communities as new forms of racial differentiation reshape community culture (Entman & Rojecki, 2000). Even when majority journalists have good intentions, desire to be sensitive, and do not discriminate consciously, their messages and lack of messages may reflect their personal cultural viewpoints that may focus on certain racial mindsets and alienate minority readers or audiences.

The multifaceted problems associated with the lack of diversity in newsrooms, as well as the lack of minority coverage that is likely to result, have been the subjects of numerous studies over the years (see e.g., Ankney & Procopio, 2003; Campbell, 1995; Entman, 1990, 1992; Jha & Izard, 2005; Mellinger, 2003; Ziegler & White, 1990). Some investigations have found positive relationships between having a diverse staff and providing community coverage. For example, it is asserted that the availability of staff members of different racial, ethnic, religious, and gender perspectives will give a news organization a wealth of story ideas that would not otherwise be available (Shipler, 1998). Moreover, nonmajority journalists are more likely than their White newsroom counterparts to question the motives for some minority coverage (Gross, Craft, Cameron, & Antecol, 2002).

A related issue, one to which researchers have paid considerable attention over the years, is the documented lack of minorities in top executive positions. It is clear, some researchers say, that this absence has a distinct impact on the coverage of minority communities and issues (see e.g., Barringer, 1999; Eisenberg, 1999; Heider, 2000; Pease & Smith, 1991; Sutton, 2000). An extensive study of minority journalists' perceptions about minority executives by Rivas-Rodriguez, Subervi-Velez, Bramlett-Solomon, and Heider (2004) found that journalists of color agree that a minority at the lead of a media operation can make positive differences in at least four ways: the news operation's sensitivity to racism, its coverage of minority groups, providing greater job opportunities for all minorities, and influencing how the news media think about minority groups.

Similarly, research on the impact of having more women in news-rooms has provided similar results. For example, Craft and Wanta (2003) examined the impact of female editors in the newsroom and found that, although the gender of editors made little difference in the issues covered, it did appear that newspapers with female editors tended to focus on positive stories and treat their female reporters on par with male reporters. In addition, Peiser's (2000) survey of German reporters indicated that women ranked social or humanitarian issues higher than did men, leading him to conclude that a higher proportion of women in newsrooms would enhance overall news judgment and media content.

Such appears to be the case with ethnic journalists, and both efforts—to improve representation among a news organization's staff and, perhaps subsequently, to broaden the scope of coverage—are believed to be positive developments for the media and in the eyes of their publics. The Gross et al. (2002) study of how Los Angeles *Times'* editorial employees and residents of Los Angeles County perceive journalists' motives for covering diverse communities shows sharp differences between journalists and residents. At the same time, however, the staff members and citizens agree that efforts to improve minority coverage reflect positively on the news organization. Furthermore, the Gross et al. study determined that the belief in the positive impact of enacting a diversity program in the *Times* newsroom suggests that, over time, this is one means by which the media may be seen by the community to be reporting fairly.

The problem of representative staffing, of course, is complex, involving years of tradition and professional newsroom practice. But the first step seems to be achieving newsroom representation that will influence community coverage. In a study of the nature of framing by the press when the risks faced by Blacks and Whites are compared, Gandy and his colleagues (1997) said that one structural influence that may be seen to influence the framing of race is the racial composition in the newsroom. They added:

> White journalists are likely to differ from their African American colleagues in the extent to which they believe individual or institutional racism is the primary influence over the outcome of some conflict. Depending on the number and influence of minority journalists within the organization, the mere presence of black journalists on staff may influence the coverage and framing of stories with a racial component. (pp. 164–165)

Gandy and his coauthors (1997) further stated the expectation that African-American and other minority journalists would be more sensitive to the racial aspects of stories. They support Gissler's (1994) belief that when minority journalists achieve a "critical mass," the character of coverage should be impacted because they will argue for or against particular slants or frames being used with stories.

Likewise, Pease, E. Smith, and Subervi (2001), in a study supported by the Poynter Institute, concluded that improvements in newsroom climate are likely to translate into the quality of the news product. When newsrooms have more diversity, they tend to provide more news about people of color than the national average. "It is intuitive to assume," they say, "the newspapers and TV operations that cover communities with greater staff diversity should reflect that diversity in their content," adding that, as a result, "improvements in newsroom climate are likely to translate into the quality of the news product" (pp. 40–41).

Most of the research on this subject presents only anecdotal evidence and has focused on minorities as a whole or on African Americans exclusively. The existing literature seems to have a dearth of empirical studies that seek to determine the relationship between Asian Americans in the newsroom and the content of their news organization. The purpose of this study is to help fill that gap.

Based on the review of the relevant literature, the researchers form the following research questions:

RQ1: Is the Asian American population in a given city related to the city paper's volume of coverage about Asian Americans?

RQ2: Is the number of Asian American staff members at a paper related to the paper's volume of coverage about Asian Americans?

RQ3: Is the number of Asian American staff members at a paper related to the Asian American population in the city where the paper is based?

RQ4: What are the topics of the stories about Asian Americans in general? Are the topics different between the papers (with more or fewer Asian American staff)?

RQ5: What are the sourcing trends of the stories about Asian Americans in general? Are sourcing trends different between the papers (with more or fewer Asian American staff)?

METHOD

To answer the aforementioned questions, several datasets were used. The researchers conducted a thorough content analysis of nine varied newspapers during June–November 2004 across the nation (some with high Asian American staff/population and some with low Asian American staff/population). All the stories published by these nine papers during the time frame were systematically sifted and selected from Lexis/Nexis. The selection of these papers was primarily based on the considerations of geographic balance and Asian American population, although a certain level of compromise was made (e.g., some papers were not available in Lexis/Nexis, so they were replaced with those that are in the region and are available). The researchers also used U.S. Census Bureau statistics to determine demographics of each of the nine cities where the papers are circulated—specifically, the percentage of the Asian American population of that city in 2005.

Additionally, we tabulated the AAJA's membership directory (of those who are currently working in the news media) to obtain an indication of the number of Asian American staff members at each paper. All nine papers were contacted to obtain demographics about the number of Asian American staff members. Unfortunately, the information provided by the nine papers varies, with the Seattle *Times* being the most cooperative and its data most detailed and other papers releasing only aggregate demographic statistics. The Boston *Globe*, New York *Times*, and Milwaukee *Journal Sentinel* declined to participate in the study primarily because of their concern for the private information involved. Because of the incomplete staff information from the papers, we decided to use the AAJA membership data of each paper to represent the number of Asian American staff. The information about each of the papers and the city's demographics are summarized in Table 4.1.

In this study, we adopted the governmental definition of *Asian Americans*, which is necessary because Census Bureau's statistics of demographics were needed for sampling and data analysis. The search for relevant news stories was conducted through Nexis/Lexis, using the

Table 4.1
Selected Papers and Key Statistics

Paper	% of Asian American Population in the City	Number of AAJA Members	Self-Reported AA Staff/Total News Staff (%)
Seattle *Times*	13.1	30	33/297 (11.1)
Los Angeles *Times*	11.1	41	80/932 (8.6)
San Diego *Union-Tribune*	13.6	12	19/394 (4.8)
Boston *Globe**	7.5	9	NA
New York *Times**	10.9	29	NA
Raleigh *News & Observer*	3.4	2	9/250 (3.6)
Milwaukee *Journal Sentinel**	3.4	2	NA
St. Louis *Post-Dispatch*	2.0	3	NA/330
Baton Rouge *Advocate*	2.6	0	0/119 (0)

*These papers declined to participate in this study, therefore, the statistic about the paper is incomplete.
NA, not available.

keywords *Asian American, Asian,* or any of the 11 Asian ethnic groups' names that exceed 1% of total Asian population in the United States in 2000 (Asian Indian, Cambodian, Chinese, Filipino, Hmong, Japanese, Korean, Laotian, Pakistani, Thai, Vietnamese) (Reeves & Burnett, 2004). When either of the keywords or any of the 11 Asian ethnicities appears in the text, that story was included in the study sample. As a second layer of the screening process, the coder read each story and decided whether it indeed related to Asian Americans, rather than exclusively to Asians internationally.

Stories that were exclusively Asian (read: geographical) were not included in the sample. It also is worth noting that the governmental definition of *Asian American* differs slightly from that of the AAJA. One major distinction is that Americans of Middle East descent are not included in the official definition of Asian American. The official definition of the Census Bureau considers Middle Eastern Americans to be White. Despite the discrepancy of definitions, the researchers screened the self-reported data of the AAJA directory and found that few AAJA members have Middle Eastern heritage. Also, none of the surveyed papers has AAJA members who are Middle Eastern Americans. Therefore, the use of AAJA members to represent Asian American staff seems justifiable.

As a result of the search and screening from the electronic archive of the nine papers, the research team found 721 stories that are relevant to Asian Americans, which are the basis of the following analysis. For each of these stories, the coders sought to document several characteristics, including:

1. by-line—Is the story written by an AAJA member, one of the Asian American staff members provided by the paper, or someone with an Asian-looking last name? Although the method is not bullet-proof, the researchers believe it is effective in providing the information needed for this study.

2. length—What is the word count of each story?

3. topics—What kinds of stories are linked to Asian Americans? Are the topics widely different or do they focus only on a limited number of subjects?

4. sources—What kinds of sources are used in the news stories? How many sources may be clearly identified as Asian Americans using the description and/or last name criteria?

5. depth—Are the stories related to Asian Americans substantive or superficial? Are the stories event-driven? Are they historically and contextually rich? Are the stories explanatory?

A story's depth is qualitative in nature, but the coding of depth can be executed in an objective, systematic fashion. For example, a story that appeared on September 9, 2004, in the San Diego *Union Tribune*, "A Land of Constant Sorrows: With 'Remains,' Seema Sueko looks for the 'truths' in painful territories," was coded "substantive" because the story covered the play by Sueko in great detail. On July 9, 2004, the San Diego paper published a short story entitled, "Daughter of Man Missing 6 Months Turns to the Public," which was coded "not substantive" because the story simply reported the basics of the incident that involved an Asian American. An August 8, 2004, story from the St. Louis *Post-Dispatch* was coded "explanatory" because the staff writer, Jerri Stroud, analyzed the directors of St. Louis area top public companies and explained the reason that women and minorities are underrepresented in that group. In contrast, the same paper on November 1, 2004, published a 168-word story entitled, "Obesity Rate in Asian Youths Is Catching Up in California." This story was rated "not explanatory" because it offered no explanation as to why the trend took place. These examples demonstrate the coding of a story's depth.

The two coders are Asian American graduate students enrolled in a public university. They went through an extensive coding training and demonstrated a satisfying level of coding. The intercoder reliability tests show that they reached perfect agreements on items such as publication date, newspaper, story length, and author's affiliation. Their agreement rate (based on Holsti's formula) on identifying story topics is 86%, and their identifications of numbers of Asian American versus other sources and paragraphs in which sources appeared in the stories (using Pearson product moment) correlate between .90 and .99. Yet their Likert-scaled assessments of story attributes (in-depth, contextual, event-driven, and explanatory) correlate only between .65 and .79 (although all with $p < .01$), indicating personal judgment was involved in coding these items. The readers might take this result into account when reading about stories' attributes in the findings section.

In addition to news coverage, this study takes the percentage of the Asian American population in each of the cities and the number of Asian American journalists working for the paper into account to examine whether patterns or trends of coverage exist relating to Asian Americans. Descriptive analyses were conducted to show the frequency and distribution of the examined variables. Moreover, both Pearson and Spearman correlation analyses between variables also were executed to examine the direction and magnitude of bivariate relationships.

FINDINGS

During the study time frame (between June and November 2004, six months before the Tsunami in South Asia), the Los Angeles *Times*, New York *Times*, and Milwaukee *Journal Sentinel* published a larger number of stories about Asian Americans than any of the other papers in the sample, followed by the Boston *Globe*, Seattle *Times*, and the San Diego *Union-Tribune*. In accordance with the findings of this study, it is not surprising that more coverage was provided by the newspapers from the cities with larger Asian American populations. Yet it is interesting to find that Milwaukee, with only 3.4% of its population Asian, published a large number of stories about Asian Americans. The comparison of the nine papers' coverage is demonstrated in Fig. 4.1. Note that the stories/population ratio in the figure was obtained from dividing the raw number of stories by a city's percentage of Asian Americans.

One of the major inquiries of this study is to determine whether the quantity of coverage about Asian Americans is—in any way—related

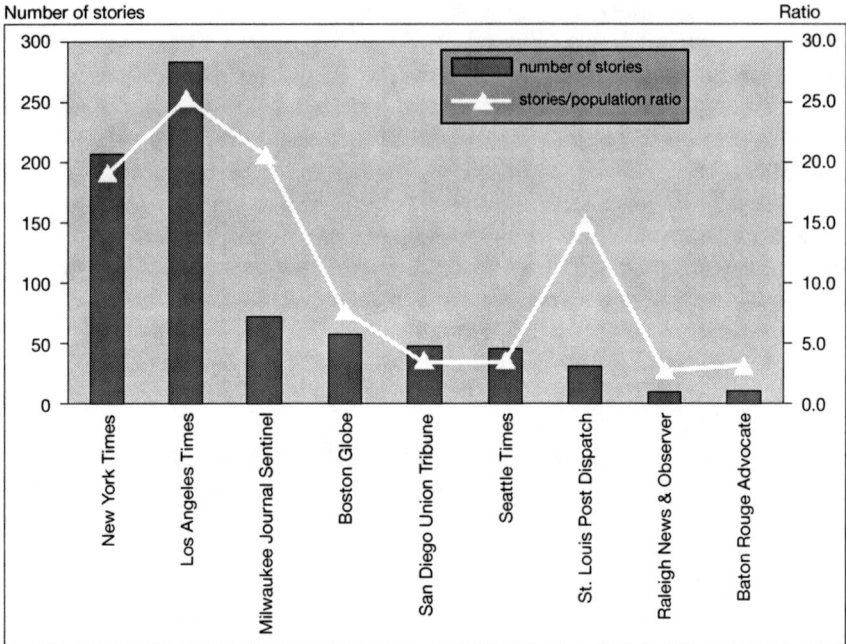

Figure 4.1. Number of stories across the nine papers.

to Asian American representation on news staffs and/or to the Asian American population in the city. The percentage of the Asian American population in a city and the numbers of stories are positively related ($r = .448$, $N = 9$, $p = .227$), although the relationship is statistically insignificant. This finding suggests that newspapers are only slightly more likely to produce stories about an ethnic group if the community includes a larger number of that group. As to the second research question, this study found that the numbers of AAJA (Asian American staff) members and the numbers of stories are positively related ($r = .818$, $N = 9$, $p = .007$). In other words, it appears clear that the more Asian American staff members a paper has, the more stories about Asian Americans it is likely to produce. This supports the content implications of having broader perspectives in the newsroom. Furthermore, the staff member–story volume correlation seems more significant (and positive) than the story volume–community relationship, which turned negative after the number of Asian American staff being controlled ($pr = .841$, $N = 6$, $p = .009$ vs. $pr = -.513$, $N = 6$, $p = .165$). This indicates that the number of staff members appears to be a stronger—and more significant—catalyst to the quantity of coverage than the factor of Asian American population.[2]

A statistically significant relationship was found between the number of AAJA members and the community's percentage of the Asian American population (r = .784, N = 9, p = .012). That newspapers with large Asian American populations were likely to have larger numbers of Asian American staff members is somewhat predictable, but nevertheless important because it does confirm conventional wisdom. These findings have shed light on the first three research questions.

Although the number of stories on Asian Americans is important to the coverage of a total community, the breadth of coverage also is indicated by topics to which attention is paid. As RQ4 asked: What kinds of stories are linked to Asian Americans? Are the topics widely different or do they focus only on a limited number of subjects? Table 4.2 summarizes the results of this phase of the analysis. Of the topics that were covered by the nine newspapers during the time frame, the greatest attention was paid to stories involving important issues of culture and entertainment and to immigration issues. There appeared to be a substantial coverage (19% of the stories) devoted to cultural events and reviews of movies, theaters, and concerts. Immigration issues, the second most prominent news topic, seemed to center on more stringent immigration procedure and issuing of student visas after September 11. Feature stories that placed spotlights on successful or prominent Asian Americans ranked third. Next, four equally notable news categories are domestic politics, crime and law enforcement, business, and food—many stories are review essays about Asian food and restaurants, especially in the New York *Times*. In addition, some attention was paid to education, social issues, and government policy.

Are these papers different in covering Asian Americans? Based on the results yielded from Spearman correlation tests of news topics across the papers, three papers of cities with substantial Asian American populations—Seattle, Boston, and San Diego—are correlated with one another significantly: Seattle–Boston, *Spearman's rho* = .784, N = 15, p = .001; Boston–San Diego, *Spearman's rho* = .796, N = 15, p < .001; San Diego–Seattle, *Spearman's rho* = .758, N = 15, p = .001. The New York and Los Angeles papers seem to resemble each other (*Spearman's rho* = .717, N = 16, p = .002), yet the former also resembles the Seattle paper, whereas

---

[2]Partial correlation (pr) indicates the net magnitude of relationship between the two examined variables controlling for the third variable. In other words, the first partial correlation coefficient shows the relationship between Asian American staff and story quantity controlling for Asian American population.

Table 4.2
Topics of News Stories About Asian Americans in Nine Papers

Topics	n	% of Appearances	% of Stories*
Culture and entertainment	137	15.0	19.1
Immigration/naturalization	97	10.7	13.5
Feature of people	88	9.7	12.2
Domestic politics	79	8.7	11.0
Crime and law enforcement	79	8.7	11.0
Food	78	8.6	10.8
Business	76	8.4	10.6
Education	59	6.5	8.2
Other	52	5.7	7.2
Social issues	42	4.6	5.8
Governmental policy	37	4.1	5.1
Sports	20	2.2	2.8
International relations	16	1.8	2.2
Economics	15	1.7	2.1
Religion	15	1.7	2.1
Travel	11	1.2	1.5
Health	4	.4	.6

Note. There are 906 topic appearances in 721 stories.
* The total of this column is more than 100% because multiple topics can exist in a story.

the latter resembles the Milwaukee *Journal-Sentinel*. Almost all of the news stories related to Asian Americans were written by staff reporters. Only about 3% came from news agencies (AP, Reuters, and Bloomberg), and 7% were contributed by freelancers. These statistics suggest that the stories about Asian Americans are predominantly local.

Another journalistic criterion of breadth of coverage of Asian Americans, or any ethnic group, is the degree to which they serve as sources of stories. In this study, it is worth noting that the sources were identified by the coder through the use of their last names and the description—if any—that accompanies the sources. This procedure admittedly has its risks, but it nevertheless provides a reasonable indication of the use of Asian Americans in the news. The results of this analysis indicate that 34% of all sources in the stories provided by the nine newspapers were identified with Asian American sources. In other words, about one third of the time, the sources of information in the stories were Asian Americans—1.14 Asian American sources per story. A similar analysis of sourcing indicates that 35% of the paragraphs with sources in these stories contained identifiable Asian American sources. The sourcing patterns among the nine papers are significantly different ($F_{8, 648}$ = 5.915, $p < .001$). Milwaukee and Los Angeles papers are significantly lower than the Boston, Seattle, and San Diego papers. When looking at the ratio of Asian American sources against all sources in the papers, one can find that the Boston, Seattle, and San Diego papers have highest ratios (ranging between 48% and 51%), and also their percentages of paragraphs with sources that contained Asian American sources are the largest (ranging between 52% and 57%).

Although this study did determine that the number of Asian American staff members is positively linked to the number of stories about Asian Americans, it also sought to determine whether the ethnicity of the author of a news story might contribute to the attributes of the story. The conventional wisdom, once again, seems supported in this case. For example, identifiable Asian American writers are slightly more likely to use Asian American sources ($r = .121$, $N = 622$, $p = .003$) when human sources were used and to provide a slightly larger number of paragraphs that included Asian-American sources ($r = .088$, $N = 622$, $p = .028$) in their stories.

Regarding the content's depth and attributes, this study executed assessments of each story's substance, contextual information, explanation, and diversity in perspectives. Additionally, it examined whether the stories are event-driven. The results show that half of the stories focused on broader issues and were not event-driven. Of the four attributes, the stories overall scored the highest in explanation ($M = 2.06$), followed by perspective diversity ($M = 1.58$), substance ($M = 1.55$), and, finally, contextual information ($M = 1.32$).

The correlation result suggests that the stories written by Asian American authors are somewhat more substantive ($r = .090$, $N = 720$, $p = .016$) and only slightly richer in story context ($r = .069$, $N = 720$, $p = .065$). However, there is no evidence indicating that Asian American writers differ from other writers in the length of their stories and in providing more diverse, explanatory, and analytical (as opposed to event-driven) perspectives into the stories. These findings are somewhat counterintuitive—perhaps newsroom custom and journalism tradition are at work.

CONCLUSION

This study supports the long-suspected association between the presence of ethnic journalists and both the quantity and attributes of reporting about an ethnic group. It appears (appropriately) that a city's Asian American population does relate to both quantity and quality of coverage provided by that city's newspaper. More important, however, it also appears to be the case that the number of Asian American staff in the newsroom is an even stronger catalyst for coverage. Certainly, this finding supports those in both the industry and the academy who advocate more minority hiring in news media. We also found a strong correlation between Asian American population and the number of Asian American staff working in the paper, which also seems to be a positive sign.

The study also shows that, overall, the topics of stories about Asian Americans tended to be evenhanded between issues and events. Although the nine papers examined indicated different concentrations of topics— with papers of big cities resembling each other more, major focus was placed on culture and entertainment, immigration issues, people profiles, and even food. The stories appeared to make reasonable use of Asian Americans as sources. On average, one in three sources in these stories pertaining to Asian Americans were Asian Americans. Regarding sourcing patterns, Asian American sources were used slightly differently among the nine papers, but the Boston, San Diego, and Seattle papers showed a higher tendency to use Asian American sources than others. Although Asian American reporters are slightly more likely to use Asian American sources and provide more substance in the stories examined, they do not necessarily produce stories that are more contextual, explanatory, or less event-driven. This interesting phenomenon is worthy of further investigation. Perhaps the industry norms and journalism tradition are a stronger force than individual efforts.

This study has several limitations. For one, the fact that some of the newspapers refused to provide their staff's demographic information to the authors makes this examination less satisfactory. The use of the AAJA directory to represent the presence of Asian American staff in the newsroom is a compromising result. Also, the method—based on the AAJA directory data, news description, and last names—used in this study to determine the ethnic background of authors and sources is far from perfect. But this is the best method the authors can use. It is not unusual that Asian Americans have non-Asian-looking/sounding last names. The newspaper industry should welcome academic, independent research such as this one and be more cooperative in the future.

The findings generated from this study might shed light on the relationships between ethnic staffing and news coverage about ethnic groups and provide evidence to support the benefit of more minority hiring in the newsroom. The link appears to be solid and significant for Asian Americans. More studies should be implemented to investigate other ethnic or minority groups to paint a more complete picture of this inquiry.

REFERENCES

Adams, T., & Cleary, J. (2006). The parity paradox: Reader response to minority newsroom staffing. *Mass Communication and Society*, 9(1), 45–61.

American Society of Newspaper Editors. (1999). *ASNE benchmarks for 2000–2025 as adopted by ASNE Board*. Available at http://www.asne.org/kiosk/diversity/benchmarksfaq.htm

American Society of Newspaper Editors. (2005). *News staffs shrinking while minority presence grows*. Available at http://www.asne.org/index.cfm?id=5648

Ankney, R. N., & Procopio, D. A. (2003). Corporate culture, minority hiring, and newspaper coverage of affirmative action. *The Howard Journal of Communications*, 14, 159–176.

Barringer, F. B. (1999, July 12). Big turnout for minority journalists conference is spirited but newsroom numbers are stagnant. *The New York Times*, p. A2.

Campbell, C. P. (1995). *Race, myth and the news*. Thousand Oaks, CA: Sage.

Craft, S., & Wanta, W. (2003) Women in the newsroom: Influences of female editors and reporters on the news agenda. *Journalism & Mass Communication Quarterly*, 81, 1.

Dedman, B., & Doig, S. K. (2005, June 1). *Newsroom diversity has passed its peak at most newspapers, 1990–2005 study shows*. Available at http://powerreporting.com/knight/

Eisenberg, P. (1999, August 8). Hiring minorities is only half the challenge. *The Freedom Forum & Newseum News*, p. 6.

Entman, R. (1990). Modern racism and the images of blacks in local television news. *Critical Studies in Mass Communication*, 7, 332–345.

Entman, R. M., & Rojecki, A. (2000). *The black image in the white mind: Media and race in America*. Chicago: University of Chicago Press.

Gandy, O. H., Jr., Kopp, K., Hands, T., Frazer, K., & Phillips, D. (1997). Race and risk: Factors affecting the framing of stories about inequality, discrimination, and just plain bad luck. *Public Opinion Quarterly*, 61(1), 158–182.

Gissler, S. (1994, Summer). Newspapers' quest for racial candor. *Media Studies Journal*, 123.

Gross, R., Craft, S., Cameron, G. T., & Antecol, M. (2002). Diversity efforts at the *Los Angeles Times*: Are journalists and the community on the same page? *Mass Communication and Society*, 5(3), 263–277.

Heider, D. (2000). *White news: Why local news programs don't cover people of color*. Mahwah, NJ: Erlbaum.

Jha, S., & Izard, R. (2005, Fall/Winter). Who got to talk about it: Sourcing and attribution in broadcast news coverage of the first 24 hours of the "9/11 Tragedy." *Seattle Journal for Social Justice*, 2(1), 101–118.

Mellinger, G. (2003, April). Counting color: Ambivalence and contradiction in the American Society of Newspaper Editors' discourse of diversity. *Journal of Communication Inquiry*, 27(2), 129–151.

Pease, T., Smith, E., & Subervi, F. (2001). *News & race: Models of excellence*. Poynter Institute. Available at http://www.poynter.org/content/content_view.asp?id=5045

Pease, T., & Smith, J. F. (1991). The newsroom barometer: Job satisfaction and the impact of racial diversity at U.S. daily newspapers. *The Ohio Journalism Monograph Series*, No. 1. E.W. Scripps School of Journalism.

Peiser, W. (2000). Setting the journalist agenda: Influences from journalists' individual characteristics and from media factors. *Journalism & Mass Communication Quarterly, 77*, 243–57.

Reeves, T. J., & Burnett, C. E. (2004, December). *We the people: Asians in the United States.* Washington, DC: U.S. Census Bureau.

Rivas-Rodriguez, M., Subervi-Velez, F. A., Bramlett-Solomon, S., & Heider, D. (2004). Minority journalists' perceptions of the impact of minority executives. *The Howard Journal of Communications, 15*, 39–55.

Shipler, D. K. (1998, May/June). Blacks in the newsroom. *Columbia Journalism Review, 37*(1), 26.

Sutton, W. (2000, April 17). Black journalists prepare for convention in Phoenix. *Arizona Republic*, p. 2.

U.S. Census Bureau. (2006). *Census bureau projects tripling of Hispanic and Asian populations in 50 years; Non-Hispanic Whites may drop to half of total population.* Available at http://www.census.gov/Press-Release/www/releases/archives/population/001720.html

Ziegler, D., & White, A. (1990). Women and minorities on network television news: An examination of correspondents and newsmakers. *Journal of Broadcasting and Electronic Media, 34*, 215–223.

Chapter 5

Constructing Asian Americans as Aliens and Outsiders: A Qualitative Analysis of Newspaper Coverage of Election Campaigns

Given the powerful influence of media on society in general and politics in particular, biased media treatment of ethnic groups, especially in the context of news coverage of election campaigns, deserves careful scrutiny. Understandably, many previous studies on racial stereotyping in entertainment and news media have focused on African Americans (e.g., Busselle & Crandall, 2002; Entman, 1990, 1992, 1994; Entman & Rojecki, 2000; Rada, 2000). News portrayal of women and African-American political candidates also has received scholars' attention (Kahn & Gordon, 1997; Nelson & Meranto, 1977; Norris, 1997; Peer & Ettema, 1998; Perry, 1996; Sylvie, 1995). Little research, however, exists on news and especially election campaign coverage of Asian Americans (Auman & Mark, 1997; Heuterman, 1997; Mansfield-Richardson, 1997), despite the improving political status and visibility of this minority group (Aoki & Nakanishi, 2001; Lai, Cho, Kim, & Takeda, 2001). The only exception we have located was a book chapter by Larson (2006), which analyzes three election campaigns.

To fill this void in the literature, we collected and examined newspaper articles on Asian American candidates and their opponents in five relatively recent elections. Analyses of such news reports will lend more insight into the overall treatment of racial minorities by the U.S. news media and will shed light on important similarities and differences in such coverage. For instance, although existing research (e.g., Entman & Rojecki, 2000) suggests that racial minorities tend to be portrayed stereotypically, it is possible that Asian Americans will be treated as somewhat foreign in comparison with African Americans. Such a finding would be consistent with the general treatment of Asian Americans historically (J. Wu & Song, 2000).

Chapter 3 is a quantitative analysis of five election campaigns involving Asian American candidates. By contrast, the current chapter identifies and qualitatively interprets the recurring themes and frames used in the portrayal of five Asian American political candidates. We have two specific objectives. The first is to analyze how these political elites were defined by mainstream news media. The second is to explore and identify the ideologies and meanings behind such coverage. In a broader sense, the findings should help the media avoid mistakes in covering racial minority candidates in future elections.

FRAMING IN THE NEWS

Our analysis of newspaper articles takes a "framing" approach, so let us begin with a review of framing literature. Language functions as a tool to shape, define, and legitimize experience, and thus it creates meanings and facilitates human understandings and interactions. In other words, language organizes and structures the world for us by assigning meanings and significance; basically language constructs reality for the reader (Corcoran, 1990; Fowler, 1991; Spender, 1980, 1984). Language in the news plays a direct and significant role in shaping social reality for many media consumers because news coverage essentially serves as their window to the world (Fowler, 1991; Kress, 1983; Lippman, 1922). Media, therefore, serve a gate-keeping function for consumers, while the necessarily selective nature of gathering and reporting news help shape social reality (Tuchman, 1978). Generally speaking, a constructed reality is subjective because the shaper provides the context for understanding by reconstructing an original event within a certain perceptual frame.

Related to how language is used to shape reality, frames can be understood as conceptual or cognitive views of particular situations (Bateson, 1972; Chenail, 1995; Goffman, 1974). Meanings are produced in the process in which information is organized in a certain way and a particular frame or context is provided (Herman, 1991; Kress, 1983). For instance, calling a "tax cut for the rich" a "tax relief" may change how voters perceive the issue in question (Lakoff, 2004). Framing in the news provides a context for meanings in which a complex issue can be simplified and understood by the audience (Entman, 1993; Gamson, 1992; Pan & Kosicki, 1993; Scheufele, 1999). That is, the news media organize stories in ways that provide meaning to news events for their readers and viewers (Andsager, 2000). Specifically, framing occurs "as journalists select some aspects of perceived reality and make it more important in their news story by promoting a particular problem, causal interpretation, or treatment recommendation" (Powers & Andsager, 1999, p. 553). Framing takes place when the direction and focus of the audience are influenced by the news media.

Media scholars have used the concept of framing to examine media coverage of such groups as political protesters, African Americans, and political interest groups, including prochoicers and prolifers (Andsager, 2000; Entman, 1990, 1992, 1994; McLeod, 1995; McLeod & Detenber, 1999). However, the ways that Asian Americans are framed in the news remain to be explored.

REASONS BEHIND NEGATIVE FRAMES

Why are negative frames used to describe certain situations and groups? Possible reasons include prejudice, stereotypes, power struggle, and ideologies. Ehrlich (1973) defines *prejudice* as an attitude, either positive or negative, toward any group of people. Such an attitude is rarely based on convincing evidence or logical reasoning. A stereotype, which is basically a cognitive shortcut, is a set of beliefs and disbeliefs (both positive and negative) about a group of people with common attributes or characteristics (Ehrlich, 1973; Waller, 1998). Beliefs often lead to attitudes. Prejudice, which is a positive or negative attitude toward others because of their group membership, does not necessarily link to behavior, but may be used to justify negative actions toward a group (Ruscher, 2001; Waller, 1998). Fowler (1991) defines *stereotype* as a "socially-constructed mental pigeonhole into which events and individuals can be sorted, thereby making such events and individuals comprehensible" (p. 17). Once one's locale on the map of power relationship is defined, others in the same power structure can understand how this person should be perceived and treated.

Imbalance frequently occurs in a power structure, and domination and submission are inevitable. Members of a dominant group utilize various means to sustain and expand their power, often by putting other people down (thus asserting their own superior location or position in the power structure) (Lukes, 1974). Ruscher (2001) points out that frequently "people lash out against outgroups [members who belong to other groups] who hold different worldviews" in order to "attest to the superiority of the ingroup's values and qualities" (p. 8). Membership in such groups, based on a variety of social constructs such as religion and race, are used to distinguish outcasts (Ruscher, 2001; Schimel et al., 1999). Prejudice and stereotypes may be—and often are—used to support a dominant group's power in a hierarchical power structure (Ruscher, 2001).

Ideology, a key factor in one's understanding of power, is a system of beliefs about how the world should work (Becker, 1984; Shoemaker & Reese, 1996). Ideology, or a worldview, influences how people see the world, how people act, and how they are related to each other (Hinich & Munger, 1994). Therefore, prejudice and stereotypes, and where one stands in a power structure, can be considered manifestations of ideology.

Peer and Ettema's (1998) study examining news coverage of four mayoral elections, which points out that race is yet another constructed reality, also notes that, by organizing "facts," news emphasizes ("frames") certain interpretations of issues while excluding others. Peer and Ettema, along with Hall (1982) and Hackett (1984), go on to argue that news is ideological because it naturalizes such frames and makes frames invisible, yet even more powerful. According to Peer and Ettema (1998), news shapes the ideological environment, which functions as "background assumptions, ideas, values, and propositions" that are "subtly embedded in the conventions of news productions" (p. 257). These researchers also see news as being ideological because it makes the audience position in a power structure by taking on a particular identity.

RACIAL STEREOTYPES AND IDEOLOGIES IN SOCIETY AND THE NEWS

People's prejudicial attitudes can be influenced by many sources, but stereotypes in media content no doubt are important. The effects of biased media content on audience learning and socialization of racial attitudes have been documented (Busselle & Crandall, 2002; Entman & Rojecki, 2000; Fujioka, 1999, 2005; Rada, 2000; Tan et al., 2001). The influence also can go the other direction: Social reality can be reflected in the media as well (Hamamoto, 1994).

Because struggles for power often occur in the real world, we can expect to find such discourse in the news because news is supposed to be a representation of the world (Fowler, 1991). To understand how reality is constructed and why a certain reality is selected over its alternatives, media scholars have examined the context of coverage, the people who produced the news, and the ideology behind the practice of coverage (Bybee, 1990; Gitlin, 1980; Herman & Chomsky, 1988; Tuchman, 1978).

The U.S. media reflect mainstream and dominant ideologies, as well as the interests of the power status quo (Altschull, 1995; Breed, 1958; Herman & Chomsky, 1988; McLeod & Detenber, 1999). As a result, "fringe" and protest groups that challenge the existing power structure are often marginalized, ridiculed, and covered in stereotypical ways by the news media (Dardis, 2006; Gitlin, 1980; McLeod, 1995; McLeod & Detenber, 1999). For example, according to some news accounts, feminists were described as "bickering" with each other at a women's summit (Danner & Walsh, 1999), and gay activists were said to be fighting among themselves in political marches (Hicks & Lee, 2001). Such reporting angles and frames reflect mainstream ideologies that promote a mentality that distrusts and marginalizes feminism and homosexuality.

Stereotypical portrayals of African Americans are rampant in the media, including the news, which continue to manifest the ideology of racism against this minority group. African Americans, according to the literature, have been inaccurately and negatively portrayed as being inferior, lazy, dishonest, violent, criminal, comical, unethical, power- and money-hungry, and ignorant (Dates, 1990; Entman, 1990, 1992, 1994; Entman & Rojecki, 2000; Martindale, 1996; Martindale & Dunlap, 1997; Rada, 2000; U.S. Commission for the Study of Civil Rights, 1977).

Among the limited amount of media research on Asian Americans, scholars have reported that media—especially news—coverage or portrayal of this group is scant and tends to be negative or even hostile (Auman & Mark, 1997; Heuterman, 1997; Hamamoto, 1994; Larson, 2006; R. Lee, 1999; Mansfield-Richardson, 1997). Such portrayals are likely related to a mainstream ideology regarding Asian Americans.

Occasionally, Asian Americans are seen as a "model minority," in part, because of their overall above average socioeconomic status (SES) and the stereotype that they are intelligent and hardworking (Auman & Mark, 1997; Wong, 1994). However, they are often considered outsiders by their fellow Americans, despite their generations of contribution to this nation (Anti-Defamation League, 2001; F. Wu, 2002). In other words, a prominent ideology about Asian Americans is that they are permanent outsiders or aliens, which leads to their disadvantaged position in a relationship network of power. This chapter is an in-depth analysis of how this ideology affects news coverage of Asian American politicians.

The following examples clearly illustrate this perpetual outsider status of Asian Americans. R. Lee (1999) reports that a White man approached him and a group of fellow Asian American scholars in a San Diego restaurant and asked them where they were from. When their answers were a number of cities in the United States, that man thought they misunderstood his question. A large national survey in 2001 reported that 25% of Americans held negative views toward Chinese Americans, and the majority of citizens would not want a Chinese-American president (Anti-Defamation League, 2001; Lyke, 2001). More recently, on August 11,

2006, at a campaign rally for his failed reelection bid, Virginia Senator George Allen called a college student of East Indian descent—who was born in the United States and a volunteer from his opponent's campaign—a "macaca" and welcomed him to America (Shear, 2006; Sherman, 2006).

This worldview or ideology concerning Asian Americans certainly has its historical roots in the not-so-distant past (Hamamoto, 1994). The Chinese Exclusion Act was passed in 1882, and the last Chinese Exclusion Extension Act was approved in 1904. The race-based immigration law was not repealed until 1943. Also, starting in 1942, more than 100,000 Japanese Americans were sent to concentration camps during World War II because their "home country" was at war with the United States (Tung, 1974; J. Wu & Song, 2000). By contrast, there was no identical treatment of this scale toward German and Italian Americans, although Germany and Italy were also enemies of the United States during this same period.

DATA

Building on the relevant research reviewed previously, the fundamental goal of the present study is to investigate whether the frame of outsiders or aliens was revealed in news coverage of Asian Americans who were major party candidates in five recent high-profile campaigns. In other words, the focus of investigation is whether and how these Asian Americans are framed as aliens in the new discourse. Specifically, the present chapter examines whether and how news stories drew attention to certain election candidates' racial and ethnic background and, if so, how any assessment of it is offered.

We selected five recent U.S. elections outside Hawaii that involved Asian Americans and had received significant national or regional media attention. The campaigns were the 1993 mayoral campaign in Los Angeles (Michael Woo vs. Richard Riordan), the 1996 gubernatorial campaign in Washington (Gary Locke vs. Ellen Craswell), the 1998 first congressional district (Portland area) election in Oregon (David Wu vs. Molly Bordonaro), the 1998 U.S. senatorial campaign in California (Matt Fong vs. Barbara Boxer), and the 2003 gubernatorial campaign in Louisiana (Piyush "Bobby" Jindal vs. Kathleen Blanco). Woo, Locke, Wu, Fong, and Jindal are Asian Americans, and Riordan, Craswell, Bordonaro, Boxer, and Blanco are all White Americans. Specifically, Woo, Locke, and Wu are Democrats and Chinese Americans, Fong is a Republican and Chinese American, and Jindal is a Republican and Indian American.

For the four campaigns in the 1990s, four newspapers were selected for analysis (the Los Angeles *Times*, Seattle *Times*, *Oregonian*, and San Francisco *Chronicle*) due to their extensive coverage of the campaigns of interest, and their importance as well as circulation in their own states (California, Washington, and Oregon). For the Louisiana race in 2003, three newspapers were used because neither appeared to be the single best source. The three papers are the Shreveport *Times*, the Baton Rouge *Advocate*, and the New Orleans *Times-Picayune*.

The study period covers the beginning of each primary to 2 days after each general election. Using specific years and names of all candidates in the general elections as keywords, relevant stories from the LA *Times*, Seattle *Times*, San Francisco *Chronicle*, and the three Louisiana papers were identified and obtained from the Lexis-Nexis and America's Newspapers databases. In the same fashion, relevant *Oregonian* articles were acquired from a CD-ROM of the newspaper at the University of Oregon library. Letters to the editor, editorials, and other opinion pieces were excluded.

Ninety-nine articles, including any racial or ethnic references of any candidate in primaries and general elections, were identified and used for this study. Seventy-eight of 99 (78.8%) stories contained racial or ethnic references about the Asian American candidates. In contrast, only eight stories (7.4%) contained racial or ethnic information exclusively about their opponents in both primary and general elections. Eleven articles (11.1%) contained such information on both the Asian American candidates and their opponents. These figures suggest that the five Asian American candidates in question received disproportional attention to their ethnic/racial backgrounds in comparison with their opponents. However, the focus of this study is how the candidates were portrayed in newspaper articles, rather than statistics of the articles (please see chap. 3 for such statistics).

Following the approach in similar qualitative studies (e.g., Gitlin, 1980; Luther, 2002), in-depth reading of all relevant articles led to the identification and further analysis of recurring themes. Quotations are used to illustrate three identified frames of news coverage.

FINDINGS

Theme 1: Asian American Candidates Are Ethnic and Exotic

An effective way to make a group "stand out" is to single it out and bring readers' attention to it. This practice is likely to remind the audience of the "fact" that this group is not part of the "ingroups."

Michael Woo is identified as "a person of color" in a February 5, 1993, Los Angeles *Times* story. In a June 6, 1993, article in the same newspaper, Woo's opponent Richard Riordan is described as a member of an "Irish-Catholic clan." In all the newspaper articles analyzed in this chapter, Riordan and Barbara Boxer are the only two White candidates whose ethnicity (Irish and Jewish) is identified.

By comparison, Fong Locke, Woo, and Wu are repeatedly labeled as Chinese American, son or grandson of Chinese immigrants, and able to become the first Asian or Chinese American to occupy the office they were running for if elected. Fong reportedly worked as a San Francisco Chinatown tour guide during his teenage years. Similarly, Jindal is repeatedly identified as Indian American, son of Indian immigrants, and a candidate with an Indian heritage, ethnicity, origin, or ancestry. Specifically, reporters clearly state that David Wu could become the first Chinese American congressman from Oregon, Locke could be the first Chinese American governor and the first Asian American governor outside of Hawaii, and Bobby Jindal could become the first Indian American and Asian American governor in Louisiana. Also, Wu was the only candidate who was not born in the United States, and his birthplace (Taiwan) was mentioned in several articles.

We understand that race and ethnicity are important facts about a potential congressman or governor, but reporters went much deeper than necessary in their coverage of these politicians. Detailed information about the culture of the candidates' ancestors is provided in those newspaper articles. For example, a June 3, 1993, Los Angeles *Times* story described Michael Woo in the following terms: "the only son of an only son of a Chinese immigrant." The article went on to discuss how important it is for a Chinese family to have a son, and how happy his family was when he was born because he had two older sisters. The story reads: "It was the first and only boy born to a traditional Chinese family that had two daughters and had prayed for a son. . . . Two more sisters followed Woo and his gender was all the reason needed for indulgence."

In the same article, Riordan's family background is mentioned: "Riordan's father was, by all accounts, a remarkable figure. A high school dropout whose parents immigrated from Ireland. . . ." Along with a short line about his mother and another stating that Riordan "revels in upper-middle class ethnicity—the church, the Friendly Sons of St. Patrick, the cardinal's inner circle," these brief details are the extent of the article's description of Riordan's family and cultural heritage.

The family and cultural heritage aspect of Michael Woo are detailed much more than that of his Irish American opponent. In another article published on the same day, Chinese philosophy and politics are mentioned: "More secular in his upbringing, shaped by the Confucian ethos,

Woo has expressed and corroborated his worth and success in life through politics and art." The same article also wrote: "To be sure, Woo's Chinese heritage has cautioned him against a total embrace of the public solution. His family, especially on his mother's side, believed in the private sector. Politically speaking, they believed in Chiang Kai-shek, not Mao Tse-tung." By contrast, no Irish politicians or philosophers are cited to suggest Riordan's capitalist mentality.

On a few occasions, depictions with a racial and ethnic overtone go beyond the coverage of the campaign trail. For instance, Gary Locke's victory celebration dinner was described this way in a November 6, 1996, Seattle *Times* story:

> Life in a Chinese family sometimes seems like a series of banquets. No event is too small or large to avoid being marked by a large meal and a gathering of the clan. Too much food is eaten. Too much of everything is drunk and too little of real substance is said. Tiny red lay see envelopes are showered on everybody in attendance.

In case you are wondering, "lay see" is Cantonese (a Chinese dialect) for red envelopes containing cash as gifts. It is clear that ethnic and "exotic" frames were employed in the reporting of the Asian American candidates. It would be easy for readers to notice that these candidates were Asian and, more specifically, Chinese or Indian American. Although three of them were native-born American, readers were encouraged to see them as foreigners. For instance, two candidates' families were portrayed as continuing to live in a Chinatown-like environment where traditional culture was well preserved. By comparison, the race or ethnicity of the opposing candidates were barely mentioned likely because their racial background is the norm and therefore a nonissue.

Although the following example is an advertisement instead of a news report, this incident illustrates how Asian Americans are perceived by some of their fellow citizens has not changed. A Baton Rouge *Advocate* (September 23, 2003) article reports a "mysterious" ad for a candidate in the New Orleans *Times-Picayune*. The headline of that advertisement reads: "Forget the Foreign and Senior Candidates and the Choice Is Clear for a Change—Jay Blossman for Governor." Apparently Bobby Jindal is called a "foreign" candidate in this advertisement. Blossman denied his sponsorship for that ad.

Theme 2: The American Dream and Model Minority

The term *American Dream* has many meanings (Cullen, 2003). For the purposes of this study, it is defined as the ideal that every person can achieve freedom, happiness, equality, and prosperity through hard work, courage, and determination. Also, as discussed earlier, the term *model minority* means a member or group of a racial or ethnic minority who is hard working, intelligent, and successful—defined, for example, as achieving a high SES. This frame is another recurring theme in the newspaper articles on the five Asian American candidates.

A September 26, 1996, Seattle *Times* story reports: "Locke talks often of his youth, growing up with immigrant parents and striving for the American dream." A November 1, 1996, article in the same paper revealed that Locke grew up in a housing project. The same story states that "he has talked often about his Chinese-immigrant parents and what he has described as a tough childhood." The same newspaper on August 22, 1996, published a story including this statement about Locke's campaign: "His stump speech tells THE great American story—immigrant-rags to citizen-riches."

In an April 26, 1998, *Oregonian* article, David Wu was described this way: "The once-shy immigrant has become a nonstop networker trying to win the Democratic primary election." This news article depicted him as: "a shy young immigrant who spoke only Chinese. He grew into an unabashed extrovert who speaks flawless English—a lot." He reportedly struggled to fit in while attending school in California and later lifted weights until he could play football. The same article states, "By his senior year, Wu was a co-captain of the football team—while taking college-level math and earning A's in German class." Later he attended college at Stanford, went on to medical school at Harvard, and then transferred to law school at Yale.

In a November 4, 1998, San Francisco *Chronicle* article about Matt Fong's concession speech, he is quoted: "Who would have thought that the great-grandson of a Chinese laborer . . . would be here as your standard-bearer tonight."

Michael Woo also was portrayed as another person who realized his American Dream. A June 3, 1993, Los Angeles *Times* article reports:

> Although Woo does not see himself as the stereotypical Asian American whiz kid, he loved to read and excelled in school. Even as a toddler, his mother said, he would push aside his toys and sit in a corner leafing through a magazine. He was never athletic and sprained his ankle "annually," as he recalls.

Bobby Jindal is identified as a Rhodes Scholar that "Louisiana is not used to" (the Shreveport *Times*, August 31, 2003). He also is called a "classic overachiever" (the Shrevrport *Times*, July 6, 2003). He ran for governor when he was 32.

Although the American Dream is supposedly for everyone, the White American candidates opposing Fong, Jindal, Locke, Woo, and Wu have not been portrayed with the same frame. In fact, their personal histories were rarely reported. There were few exceptions. For instance, Gary Locke's opponent Ellen Craswell was reportedly a conservative Christian, and Michael Woo's opponent was called a rich businessman. In addition, an October 4, 1998, *Oregonian* story reports that Molly Bordonaro, David Wu's opponent, majored in English in college and that her father was a businessman. Another article in the same paper published on April 28, 1998, stated that Bordonaro went to Lincoln High School, her grandfathers were "prominent Portland residents," and her father helped build the Vietnam Memorial in Washington Park in Portland. From a few articles, readers learn that Kathleen Blanco has a husband who was working in the University of Louisiana system. Only once Barbara Boxer was briefly identified as Jewish in a July 16, 1998 article in the San Francisco *Chronicle*. These are among the few stories in which the White American candidates' personal history, background, or family are ever discussed.

Political candidates often try hard to persuade the news media to portray them in a certain (positive) manner, but they do not always succeed. Gary Locke and Michael Woo might have invited attention to the immigrant background of their parents and grandparents. However, newspapers reporters chose to adopt and further develop this frame by describing how the Asian American candidates overcame various hardships while growing up and became successful. By contrast, the journalists did not cover the White American candidates in the same manner. Regardless of the sources of information or reporters' motivation, the American Dream and model minority is the second recurring frame that news stories used in portraying the Asian American candidates, thus differentiating them from their White counterparts.

Theme 3: Support and Fighting Among Their "Own Kind" and Tension Between Racial Groups

The news media have the tendency to decide whether a candidate has the potential to be elected, and such decisions help determine how much coverage a particular candidate would receive later (Meyrowitz, 1992, 1994). One way to declare whether a candidate is viable is to analyze his or her support base. A November 1, 1996, Seattle *Times* story described Gary Locke's fundraising effort this way: "His heritage has produced financial rewards for the campaign. Locke raised tens of thousands of dollars from Asian Americans around the country." Similarly, on April 22, 1998, the *Oregonian* reported that David Wu received financial contributions from Chinese Americans, whereas his opponent Molly Bordonaro received donations from a women's group. The same article's headline read "Wu defends Chinese American donations" and stated that Wu accused his opponent in the Democratic primary, Linda Peters, of "trying to 'poison the well' by highlighting that aspect" of his financial support.

On October 13, 1996, a Seattle *Times* story discussed Locke's financial support: "Locke's latest reports show Microsoft founder Bill Gates and his wife, Melinda, have each donated $1,100; thousands of dollars from seafood companies; $1,100 from the statewide police association; union money; and thousands from Asian Americans from across the country." No word about Locke's opponents receiving political contributions from any ethnic groups.

The headline of a July 31, 2003, *Times-Picayune* article read: "Jindal's candidacy thrills local Indians." An October 10, 2003, story in the same newspaper stated that Jindal "has raised plenty of campaign cash from contributors who share his Indian heritage." Several other articles reported that he traveled to California to attend fundraisers targeting Indian Americans.

As for potential votes from various racial and ethnic groups, a Los Angeles *Times* article on March 20, 1993, reported: "Woo is portrayed as a panderer who makes extravagant promises to every minority group in town while Riordan is depicted as a plutocrat who is trying to buy the election." However, the same article also suggested that Woo's effort may not pay off: "Although Woo has been campaigning as the candidate best equipped to reunite what he frequently describes as a segregated city, the poll provides evidence that racial and geographic divisions may not be as sharp as people think."

Woo's support from minority groups is also analyzed in a Los Angeles *Times* story on February 5, 1993: "Drawing broad support from African-Americans, Latinos and Anglo liberals, City Councilman Michael Woo has moved well ahead of the field in the Los Angeles mayor's race, while the rest of the pack tries to fight its way out of political obscurity." Later in the same article it read,

> The son of Chinese immigrants, Woo has considerably more voter support right now in the African-American community than do either of the prominent black candidates in the race, Holden and lawyer Stan Sanders. Similarly, Woo is doing much better among Latino voters than either of the two best-known Latino candidates,

Julian Nava, a college history professor and former U.S. ambassador to Mexico, and Linda Griego, a businesswoman and former deputy mayor for economic development.

Statements such as these may leave readers with the impression that there was some sort of racial warfare in this campaign. Two days later, on February 7, 1993, the same theme appeared in another news story: "The Los Angeles mayoral primary is shaping up as two separate contests for the votes of two separate electorates—one primarily white, the other primarily non-white. . . . Councilman Michael Woo has the lead, built largely on backing from non-white voters." This seems to suggest serious racial division and tension in Los Angeles and that White voters would not support Woo.

Covering Gary Locke's campaign, a Seattle *Times* story on September 15, 1996, pointed out that Locke is running for an office in a state "whose population is 87 percent white." The state's "overwhelmingly white electorate" was again mentioned in an October 2, 1996, article in the same newspaper. It also quoted the analysis of a political scientist on racial politics in the state of Washington:

> Even to get elected to local offices or the Legislature here, minority politicians must attract a wide spectrum of voters. Race is always there. But it isn't the great fault line as it is in the South or California. Whites aren't nervous that this politician will only represent blacks or Asians. I get the sense the divisions here are more urban-rural or urban-suburban.

Despite its face value of being beyond racial lines, this type of comment may still introduce or reinforce a sense of apprehension that Whites may have if Locke were elected.

Being Asian American in a state with a significant Asian American population may work to one's advantage. In the 1998 senatorial campaign, according to San Francisco *Chronicle* stories, Matt Fong attended several fundraisers sponsored by Asian American groups. At the same time, Barbara Boxer reportedly made an effort to persuade Asian Americans to vote for her instead of Matt Fong.

In a different political environment, being a racial minority can be a problem. Several articles on the Louisiana campaign discuss whether Jindal's ethnicity or "roots" would help or hurt his election. Reportedly, he, his campaign staff, and a major supporter (the departing governor Mike Foster) have downplayed the importance of his race. For instance, Mike Foster is quoted in an article in the *Advocate* (September 10, 2003) saying that Jindal is "about as American as apple pie." However, some news analyses point out that Jindal was supported by White and conservative voters, and his opponent Kathleen Blanco would win among African Americans and women. On the other hand, one reporter argues that Jindal could offer something his opponent could not—his minority status, which suggests that he would attract minority voters who would "see someone with dark skin can rise to the top in this white-dominated society" (the *Advocate*, November 11, 2003). Additionally, in an article in the *Advocate* (October 7, 2003), the journalist argues that "The conventional political wisdom ran along this line: Jindal's too dark for white voters and too light for black voters."

The prior examples illustrate that these campaigns were framed as competition between races. Specifically, the newspaper articles seem to suggest that the first four Asian American candidates would likely receive only, or more, minority votes; at the same time, their ethnic background could or should make some White voters alert and apprehensive. Bobby Jindal, in contrast, would not receive enough support from either Black or White voters because of his skin color. Therefore, these candidates' race or ethnicity was a core issue on which readers were prompted to focus in those campaigns.

CONCLUSION

Possible Framing Effects

The previous analysis demonstrates that what was presented to newspaper readers was classic framing because certain aspects—racial, ethnic, and cultural—were emphasized for some candidates and not for others. As a result, readers of the news stories examined earlier were encouraged to understand the actual complexity of an election campaign in a simple and limited way.

These news stories of Asian American elites manifest the ideology that Asian Americans are permanent aliens or outsiders. This finding echoes Larson's (2006) conclusion that news coverage of Asian American candidates tends to be "racialized" and these politicians tend to be portrayed as "always foreign." The five election campaigns we have analyzed were partially defined by the media as contests between "outsiders" versus "insiders." The news reports reinforced the notion that candidates from this minority group were "different from us" and would never become "part of us."

The five White candidates opposing Woo, Locke, Wu, Fong, and Jindal in the general or run-off elections were treated as the "ingroup" because their racial or ethnic background were rarely mentioned, except for a couple of occasions in which Richard Riordan was identified as Irish American and Barbara Boxer was identified as Jewish. Besides Woo, Locke, Wu, Fong, and Jindal, racial references in the newspaper articles were used in discussions of African American candidates and one Lebanese candidate in the primaries. This phenomenon may be explained by a journalistic tradition: The norm is *not* newsworthy. Only the unusual qualifies as news. The recurring references to the ethnicity of Woo, Locke, Wu, Fong, and Jindal suggest that being an Asian American political candidate is not "normal" and, at a deeper level, imply that they are unusual and therefore should be subject to particular suspicion.

Counterarguments

First of all, we acknowledge that newspaper articles do not represent all news media content. Also, the articles containing candidates' racial or ethnic backgrounds account for only a small portion of the campaign coverage in question. However, we argue that anyone who followed the campaigns in the newspapers would likely encounter some of the reports and, therefore, would be reminded of the "differences" of Asian American candidates. To understand the hows and whys of such differences is the focus of this chapter.

Indeed, some of the Asian American candidates may have been forthcoming about their family heritage, which in turn may have invited attention to their ethnicity. However, journalists seemed to be interested in unveiling the "uniqueness" of Asian American candidates even when the candidates likely did not mention it. For instance, a few newspaper articles discuss the influence of Chinese philosophers and politicians on the candidates' families and themselves, indicate how the candidate was treated differently from his siblings, and provide detailed descriptions of a "typical" Chinese family dinner involving such foreign phrases as "lay see envelopes." Although there is no reason to hide such "facts" about these candidates, one could easily question why White candidates in the same campaigns have not received similar attention about their own unique ethnic and family attributes.

These five campaigns were political races in which all candidates are supposed to be different but equal. All the candidates are citizens of the United States, although they have different political views and policy positions. There are many potential frames and angles from which journalists may choose. The articles analyzed in this study, however, consistently (although not frequently) returned to the same racial and ethnic frame, which is basically a frame of "outsiders" and "aliens." When such influences as China's Chairman Mao and General Chiang are mentioned, an election is arguably constructed and framed, at least partially, as battles between "true Americans" versus aliens and their foreign influences. The underlying ideology behind such a chosen frame is therefore a mentality or ideology that treats Asian Americans as outsiders and foreigners. Such news discourse encourages readers to understand the five campaigns—by the way facts were selected and organized—as events in which candidates' race and ethnicity are legitimate and even salient issues.

If a candidate's race or ethnicity was a legitimate or even important issue, then there should be no reason to draw attention to this attribute of Michael Woo, Gary Locke, David Wu, Matt Fong, and Bobby Jindal while ignoring the same information about Richard Riordan, Ellen Craswell, Molly Bordonaro, Barbara Boxer, and Kathleen Blanco. A reasonable explanation for this discrepancy is that, although the journalists might have done so unintentionally, they probably considered these Asian Americans to be outsiders and aliens despite the fact that these candidates are U.S. citizens and represent major political parties. Therefore, these reporters function as part of a dominant ideology that treats Asian Americans as perennial outsiders.

It is possible that reporters were trying to celebrate diversity by pointing out the difference or uniqueness of these five candidates. Unfortunately, the news reports analyzed did not necessarily promote understanding, acceptance, and harmony as a diversity campaign is supposed to do. Such terms as *lay see* and Chiang Kai-shek were likely to remind readers of the "exotic" and "alien" influence that Asian American candidates could bring to public offices if elected. The third recurring theme of racial tension further supports this argument. Therefore, such news coverage likely promoted the idea that these Asian American candidates, if elected, may not understand, represent, or even serve the interests of all—especially White—voters.

Racial Stereotyping

Another important frame to be further examined is racial stereotyping. There is a long list of positive and negative stereotypes associated with Asians and Asian Americans in the U.S. Besides being a model minority, as mentioned earlier, examples include being greedy, cheap, overachieving, shy, submissive, good at math and science, and unathletic (Fong, 1998; Kitano & Daniels, 2001; R. Lee, 1999; Wong, 1994). Probably because such stereotypes are part of a larger picture of the "outsider" ideology, some of them appeared in the news stories. For instance, David Wu received straight As in high school and went to Stanford, Harvard, and Yale. Also, both he and Locke won uphill battles and overcame harsh realities from their childhoods. According to a news article, Michael Woo was not a "stereotypical Asian American whiz kid." Still, he "loved to read and excelled in school." As a toddler, he would push aside a toy to leaf through a magazine and was "never athletic and sprained his ankle annually." In addition, Bobby Jindal is called a "classic overachiever." It is hard to be more stereotypical than in such portrayals.

One might ask why fitting positive stereotypes is not desirable. As pointed out by Ruscher (2001), being smart and intelligent can be dangerous to "the rest of us." For example, being a smart "outsider" who is a U.S. citizen and a nuclear scientist, like Wen Ho Lee, is not always perceived as being a good thing because his loyalty to the United States was questioned (W. Lee & Zia, 2002). As for the frame of "the American Dream," one implication is that such a "if you work hard enough you will succeed" dream cannot, or is difficult to, be realized in foreign countries. The belief that such a dream can only come true in America demonstrates a sense of superiority associated with "ingroups."

As mentioned earlier, Peer and Ettema (1998) argued that campaign coverage is ideological, although their focus was on other aspects such as "its uncritical acceptance of race and ethnicity as appropriate tools of practical electoral politics" (p. 273). By contrast, the argument of the present study is that campaign coverage in these cases reveals the ideology of race because of such coverage's racial and ethnic frames. Also, those frames appeared with such frequency that they induced "uncritical acceptance" by readers. We believe that the uncritical acceptance of racial stereotyping or a sense of ingroup superiority are problematic in a democracy.

Can Asian Americans Become Mainstream or Part of the Ingroups?

Will Asian Americans ever become "mainstream," and therefore part of the "ingroups"? Winning elections or joining the American Olympic team is still not enough to make one an "insider" or "true American." As reported by Aoki and Nakanishi (2001), after David Wu was elected to Congress, he was denied entrance to the U.S. Department of Energy headquarters where he was to deliver a speech. His congressional identification card did not convince security guards that he was a U.S. citizen. Being a celebrity may not help either. An MSNBC website headline in

1998 read "American Beats Out Kwan" when Tara Lipinski won an Olympic figure skating gold medal even though Michelle Kwan, who placed second, is a U.S. citizen from California (Lyke, 2001). Four years later, the Seattle *Times* made the same mistake (Fancher, 2002). When Sarah Hughes defeated Kwan in the 2002 Olympic Winter Games, a Seattle *Times* subheadline read: "American outshines Kwan, Slutskaya in skating surprise." Neither headline used the term *fellow American*, implying Kwan was not American. These examples illustrate two points. First, many Americans still do not—at least, instantaneously—see Asian Americans as their fellow citizens. Second, the news media, likely unintentionally, are not helping to improve the situation.

Further Discussions

Although the model minority and American Dream frames appear to be positive on the surface, we do not advise Asian American candidates to invite the press to cover them from this perspective. The reason is obvious after reading this chapter. Journalists would likely go much deeper in this theme and the outcome would be undesirable.

Throughout the analyzed texts, we see how race and ethnicity are constructed. Racial and ethnic labels are repeatedly placed on certain candidates, but rarely on others. Also, the homelands of their ancestors are identified. In addition, foreign words, names, and customs are introduced. The "outsider" image of the five candidates (and other members of their groups) was constructed and strengthened layer after layer in the news. Newspaper readers can easily be encouraged through framing to observe and understand these campaigns as a battle between races and ethnic groups, as well as between "true Americans" versus candidates of foreign origin and whose influences should not be trusted.

A limitation of the present study is that only newspaper coverage of five campaigns is analyzed. Like many other qualitative studies, however, the focus is understanding meanings and ideologies, rather than representativeness or predictions. Another limitation of this study is the fact that it may be questionable for a content analysis study to discuss effects on the audience. Nevertheless, as pointed out by McLeod and Detenber (1999), framing could affect an audience's understanding and opinions on issues—a view shared by many other scholars (e.g., Iyengar, 1991; Price, Tewksbury, & Powers, 1997; Rhee, 1997; Shah, Domke, & Wackman, 1996). Therefore, it is acceptable to discuss possible implications of the frames in the analyzed stories as well as the ideology behind them. Future studies are encouraged to use other methods to directly measure the effects on audiences of stereotypical news coverage with ethnic references.

One more weakness of this qualitative study is of a quantitative nature. We examined five campaigns together to identify common themes. However, each election was unique. They took place in several states in different years. They also represented different types of offices. It was probably advantageous for some Asian American candidates to remind voters of their racial or ethnic backgrounds, and thus invited media attention of such characteristics. However, we argue that the real issue across campaigns was the same: whether certain candidates were depicted as outsiders or aliens. As pointed out earlier, we believe that certain news reports went way too far by portraying some candidates as exotic and foreign which might have influenced election results.

It can be concluded that news, a powerful institution that socializes its audience, supports and strengthens the ideology of insiders versus outsiders as illustrated in the examples analyzed in this chapter. In other words, language in the news media was employed in a way that upholds the status quo and designates a certain group of citizens as outsiders. As a result, at least in a symbolic way, these citizens are denied the right of being equal members of our democratic society. Such news coverage certainly creates unfair obstacles to Asian Americans who wish to participate in the political process.

As quoted by Auman and Mark (1997), Wilson and Gutierrez (1985) described five stages of how the U.S. news media had portrayed racial minorities after the 1830s: exclusion, threat, confrontation, stereotypical selection, and integration. Judging by the findings of the present study, news coverage of Asian Americans—as exemplified by media coverage of five high-profile Asian American political campaigns—still stalls in the third and fourth stages.

Understanding and acknowledging a problem is the first step toward reaching a solution. Researchers have reported various forms of injustice in media content and discussed their implications. For example, Entman and Rojecki (2000) reported that African Americans were overrepresented as criminals and underrepresented as victims. This and other media portrayals of African Americans, they argued, have increased White Americans' negative emotions toward African Americans.

With pressure from activists, along with the help of research by communication scholars, gradually the media have become more mindful about what they offer to their audiences. For example, nowadays, both print and TV news reports are less likely to mention the racial or ethnic backgrounds of criminals. It is our hope that this chapter can help reporters avoid similar mistakes in their coverage of Asian American candidates in the future and can help audiences not to be influenced by damaging reports of their fellow Americans.

REFERENCES

Altschull, J. H. (1995). *Agents of power: The media and public policy*. White Plains, NY: Longman.

Andsager, J. L. (2000). How interest groups attempt to shape public opinion with competing news frames. *Journalism and Mass Communication Quarterly, 77*, 577–592.

Anti-Defamation League (2001, April 25). *American attitudes towards Chinese Americans and Asian Americans*. Retrieved October 2, 2002, from http://www.adl. org/misc/american_attitudes_towards_hinese.asp

Aoki, A. L., & Nakanishi, D. T. (2001, September). Asian Pacific Americans and the new minority politics. *PS: Political Science and Politics*, pp. 605–610.

Auman, A. E., & Mark, G. Y. (1997). The Chinese Americans. In A. D. Keever, C. Martindale, & M. A. Weston (Eds.), *U.S. News coverage of racial minorities* (pp. 191–215). Westport, CT: Greenwood.

Bateson, G. (1972). *Steps to an ecology of mind*. New York: Ballentine Books.

Becker, S. (1984). Marxist approaches to media studies: The British experience. *Critical Studies in Mass Communication, 1*, 66–80.

Breed, W. (1958). Mass communication and socio-cultural integration. *Social Forces, 37*, 109–116.

Busselle, R., & Crandall, H. (2002). Television viewing and perceptions about race differences in socioeconomic success. *Journal of Broadcasting and Electronic Media, 46*, 265–282.

Bybee, C. (1990). Construct women as authorities: Local journalism and the microphysics of power. *Critical Studies in Media Communication, 7*, 197–214.

Chenail, R. J. (1995). Recursive frame analysis. *The Qualitative Report 2*(2). Retrieved September 30, 2002, from http://www.nova.edu/ssss/QR/ QR2-2/rfa.html

Corcoran, P. (1990). Language and politics. In D. Swanson (Ed.), *New directions in political communication* (pp. 51–86). Beverly Hills, CA: Sage.

Cullen, J. (2003). *The American dream: A short story of an idea that shaped a nation*. Oxford, UK: Oxford University Press.

Danner, L., & Walsh, S. (1999). Radical feminists and "bickering" women: Backlash in U.S. media coverage of the United Nations Fourth World Conference on Women. *Critical Studies in Mass Communication, 16*(1), 63–84.

Dardis, F. E. (2006). Marginalization devices in U.S. press coverage of Iraq War protest: A content analysis. *Mass Communication & Society, 9*(2), 117–135.

Dates, J. (1990). A war of images. In J. Dates & W. Barlow (Eds.), *Split images: African Americans in the mass media* (pp. 1–25). Washington, DC: Howard University Press.

Ehrlich, H. J. (1973). *The social psychology of prejudice: A systematic theoretical review and prepositional inventory of the American social psychological study of prejudice*. New York: Wiley.

Entman, R. M. (1990). Modern racism and the images of blacks in local television news. *Critical Studies in Mass Communication, 7*, 332–345.

Entman, R. M. (1992). Blacks in the news: Television modern racism and cultural change. *Journalism Quarterly, 69*, 341–361.

Entman, R. M. (1993). Framing: Toward clarification of a fractured paradigm. *Journal of Communication, 43*(4), 51–55.

Entman, R. M. (1994). Representation and reality in the portrayal of blacks on network television news. *Journalism Quarterly, 71*, 509–520.

Entman, R. M., & Rojecki, A. (2000) *The black image in the white mind: Media and race in America*. Chicago, IL: University of Chicago Press.

Fancher, M. R. (2002, March 3). Time won't forget readers' reminder on Kwan headline. *Seattle Times*, p. A2.

Fong, T. P. (1998). *The contemporary Asian American experience: Beyond the model minority*. Upper Saddle River, NJ: Prentice-Hall.

Fowler, R. (1991). *Language in the news: Discourse and ideology in the press*. New York: Routledge.

Fujioka, Y. (1999). Television portrayals and African-American stereotypes: Examination of television effects when direct contact is lacking. *Journalism & Mass Communication Quarterly, 76*, 52–75.

Fujioka, Y. (2005). Black media images as a perceived threat to African-American ethnic identity: Coping responses, perceived public perception, and attitudes toward Affirmative action. *Journal of Broadcasting & Electronic Media, 49*, 450–467.

Gamson, W. A. (1992). *Talking politics*. Cambridge, UK: Cambridge University Press.

Gitlin, T. (1980). *The whole world is watching: News media in the making and unmaking of the new left*. Berkeley: University of California Press.

Goffman, E. (1974). *Frame analysis: An essay on the organization of experience*. Cambridge, MA: Harvard University Press.

Hackett, R. A. (1984). Decline of a paradigm? Bias and objectivity in news media studies. *Critical Studies in Mass Communication, 1*(3), 229–259.

Hall, S. (1982). The rediscovery of ideology: Return to the repressed in media studies. In M. Gurevitch, T. Bennett, J. Curran, & J. Wollacott (Eds.), *Culture, society and the media* (pp. 56–90). London, UK: Methuen.

Hamamoto, D. Y. (1994). *Monitored peril: Asian Americans and the politics of TV representation*. Minneapolis: University of Minnesota Press.

Herman, E. (1991, January). Gulfspeak. *Z Magazine*, pp. 46–99.

Herman, E., & Chomsky, N. (1988). *Manufacturing consent: The political economy of the mass media*. New York: Pantheon.

Heuterman, T. H. (1997). The Japanese Americans. In A. D. Keever, C. Martindale, & M. A. Weston (Eds.), *U.S. news coverage of racial minorities* (pp. 216–248). Westport, CT: Greenwood.

Hicks, G., &, Lee, T. (2001, May). *Traditional newsworthiness standards and the not-so-standard event: An analysis of newspaper coverage of four Marches on Washington.* Paper presented at the annual meeting of the International Communication Association, Washington, DC.

Hinich, M. J., & Munger, M. C. (1994). *Ideology and the theory of political choice.* Ann Arbor: University of Michigan Press.

Iyengar, S. (1991). *Is anyone responsible? How television frames political issues.* Chicago, IL: University of Chicago Press.

Kahn, K. F., & Gordon, A. (1997). How women campaign for the U.S. senate: Substance and strategy. In P. Norris (Ed.), *Women, media and politics* (pp. 59–76). Oxford, UK: Oxford University Press.

Kitano, H. H. L., & Daniels, R. (2001). *Asian Americans: Emerging minorities* (3rd ed.). Upper Saddle River, NJ: Prentice-Hall.

Kress, G. (1983). Linguistic and ideological transformations in news reporting. In H. Davids & P. Walton (Eds.), *Language, image, media* (pp. 120–138). New York: St. Martin's Press.

Lai, J. S., Cho, W. K. T., Kim, T. P., & Takeda, O. (2001, September). Asian Pacific-American campaigns, elections, and elected officials. *PS: Political Science and Politics*, pp. 611–617.

Lakoff, G. (2004). *Don't think of an elephant: Know your values and frame the debate—The essential guide for progressives.* White River Junction, VT: Chelsea Green Publishing Company.

Larson, S. G. (2006). *Media & minorities: The politics of race in news and entertainment.* Lanham, MD: Rowman & Littlefield.

Lee, R. G. (1999). *Orientals: Asian Americans in popular culture.* Philadelphia, PA: Temple University Press.

Lee, W. H., & Zia, H. (2002). *My country versus me: The first-hand account by the Los Alamos scientist who was falsely accused of being a spy.* New York: Hyperion.

Lippman, W. (1922). *Public opinion.* New York: Macmillan.

Lukes, S. (1974). *Power: A radical view.* New York: Macmillan.

Luther, C. A. (2002). National identities, structure, and press images of nations: The case of Japan and the United States. *Mass Communication and Society, 5*, 57–85.

Lyke, M. L. (2001, May 24). Japanese Americans on alert for movie backlash. *Seattle Post-Intelligencer*, p. A1.

Mansfield-Richardson, V. (1997). The Asian Americans. In A. D. Keever, C. Martindale, & M. A. Weston (Eds.), *U.S. news coverage of racial minorities* (pp. 249–259). Westport, CT: Greenwood.

Martindale, C. (1996). Newspaper stereotypes of African Americans. In P. M. Lester (Ed.), *Images that injure: Pictorial stereotypes in the media* (pp. 21–25). Westport, CT: Praeger.

Martindale, C., & Dunlap, L. R. (1997). The African Americans. In A. D. Keever, C. Martindale, & M. A. Weston (Eds.), *U.S. news coverage of racial minorities* (pp. 63–145). Westport, CT: Greenwood.

McLeod, D. M. (1995). Communicating deviance: The effects of television news coverage of social protest. *Journal of Broadcasting and Electronic Media, 39*(1), 4–19.

McLeod, D. M., & Detenber, B. H. (1999). Framing effects of television news coverage of social protest. *Journal of Communication, 49*(3), 3–23.

Meyrowitz, J. (1992, March/April). The press rejects a candidate. *Columbia Journalism Review*, pp. 46–48.

Meyrowitz, J. (1994). Visible and invisible candidates: A case study in "competing logics" of campaign coverage. *Political Communication, 11*(2), 145–164.

Nelson, W. E., Jr., & Meranto, P. J. (1977). *Electing black majors: Political action in the black community.* Columbus: Ohio State University Press.

Norris, P. (Ed.). (1997). *Women, media, and politics.* Oxford, UK: Oxford University Press.

Pan, Z., & Kosicki, G. M. (1993). Framing analysis: An approach to news discourse. *Political Communication, 10*, 55–75.

Peer, L., & Ettema, J. S. (1998). The mayor's race: Campaign coverage and the discourse of race in America's three largest cities. *Critical Studies in Media Communication, 15*, 255–278.

Perry, H. L. (1996). *Race, politics, and governance in the United States.* Gainesville: University Press of Florida.

Powers, A., & Andsager, J. L. (1999). How newspapers framed breast implants in the 1990s. *Journalism and Mass Communication Quarterly, 76*, 551–564.

Price, V., Tewksbury, D., & Powers, E. (1997). Switching trains of thought: The impact of news frames on readers' cognitive response. *Communication Research, 24*, 481–506.

Rada, J. A. (2000). A new piece of the puzzle: Examining effects of television portrayals of African Americans. *Journal of Broadcasting and Electronic Media, 44*, 704–715.

Rhee, J. W. (1997). Strategy and issue frames in election campaign coverage: A social cognition account of framing effects. *Journal of Communication, 47*(3), 26–48.

Ruscher, J. B. (2001). *Prejudiced communication: A social psychological perspective.* New York: Guilford.

Scheufele, D. A. (1999). Framing as a theory of media effects. *Journal of Communication, 49*(1), 103–122.

Schimel, J., Simon, L., Greenberg, J., Pyszczynski, T., Solomon, S., Waxmonsky, J., & Arndt, J. (1999). Stereotypes and terror management: Evidence that mortality salience enhances stereotypic thinking and preferences. *Journal of Personality and Social Psychology, 77*, 905–927.

Shah, D., Domke, D., & Wackman, D. (1996). To thine own self be true: Values, framing, and voter decision-making strategies. *Communication Research, 23*, 509–560.

Shear, M. D. (2006, November 2). Vote on senate nears after tumultuous campaign controversies bury the issues in final months. *Washington Post*, p. T3.

Sherman, J. (2006, November 5). The most unfortunate use of an obscure name of a genus of monkeys—the senator from Virginia and the "macaca" heard 'round the world. *Pittsburgh (PA) Post-Gazette*, p. H6.

Shoemaker, P., & Reese, S. D. (1996). *Mediating the message: Theories of influences on mass media content* (2nd ed.). New York: Longman.

Spender, D. (1980). *Man made language*. London, UK: Routledge & Kegan Paul.

Spender, D. (1984). Defining reality. In C. Kramarae, M. Schulz, & W. M. O'Barr (Eds.), *Language and power* (pp. 195–205). Beverly Hills, CA: Sage.

Sylvie, G. (1995). Black mayoral candidates and the press: Running for coverage. *Howard Journal of Communications, 6*, 89–101,

Tan, A., Tan, G., Avdeyeva, T., Crandall, H., Fukushi, Y., Nyandwi, A., Chin, H., Wu, C., & Fujioka, Y. (2001). Changing negative racial stereotypes: The influence of normative peer information. *Howard Journal of Communications, 12*(3), 171–180.

Tuchman, G. (1978). *Making news: A study in the construction of reality*. New York: The Free Press.

Tung, W. (1974). *The Chinese in America*. Dobbs Ferry, NY: Oceana Publications.

U.S. Commission for the Study of Civil Rights. (1977). *Window dressing on the set: Women and minorities in television*. Washington, DC: U.S. Government.

Waller, J. (1998). *Face to face: The changing state of racism across America*. Cambridge, MA: Perseus.

Wilson, C. C. II, & Gutierrez, F. (1985). *Minorities and media: Diversity and the end of mass communication*. Beverly Hills, CA: Sage.

Wong, W. (1994). Covering the invisible "model minority." *Media Studies Journal, 8*(3), 49–59.

Wu, F. H. (2002). *Yellow*. New York: Basic Books.

Wu, J. Y. S., & Song, M. (2000). *Asian American studies: A reader*. New Brunswick, NJ: Rutgers University Press.

Chapter 6

Views from the Campaigns: Interviews with the Veterans Involved in the Races

Throughout this book, we have taken different paths and angles to better understand what Asian American candidates have faced during their campaigns to gain gubernatorial or congressional offices. The other chapters have tackled media coverage generated from the races, uncovered public opinion shifts and moves under assorted circumstances, detected media use patterns among ethnic groups in the United States, and examined the electability of candidates by gender and race under fictional situations (although their credentials and experiences are identical). This chapter reports on a series of interviews conducted by the authors with the public office seekers, their strategists and campaign aides, and a reporter. Contextual information derived from other sources, such as news coverage and experts' insights published in the media, was also used to extrapolate synthesis of the findings. The primary purposes of this endeavor are to unveil their campaign stories using the candidates' own words and perspectives and to present findings that other chapters, which presented findings from other research methods, might have missed.

To obtain more detailed and rich information about the various campaigns run in the past 10 years by and for Matt Fong, Piyush "Bobby" Jindal, Gary Locke, and David Wu, we contacted all the candidates, their various campaign staffs, and local reporters who covered these races. We were able to talk to Locke and Wu at length on the phone and had an in-person interview with Fong in Boston. In addition, we interviewed campaign staff members of Jindal, Locke, and Wu (Luke Letlow, Blair Butterworth, and Jeston Black, respectively) and asked them to recapitulate the most significant events, successful strategies, and salient issues during their campaigns. Finally, we contacted Chris Frink, an *Advocate* political reporter (based in Baton Rouge, Louisiana), who had covered Jindal's 2003 gubernatorial campaign and had written an inside story about covering the campaign. All the interviews were conducted by the first author of this book during the period of 2003–2005.

This list of interviewees is certainly incomplete. We wish we had been able to talk to more people to get a better sense of the commonalities and/or contrasts among party line, geographic regions, different Asian ethnicities, or even genders of candidates. But, in keeping with the goal of this book, we focused on Asian American candidates who ran for congressional or gubernatorial offices across the nation between 1990 and 2003. The number of these candidates is undoubtedly small. According to the data we were able to collect, all candidates who ran for offices at this level were male. Because we only concentrated on the races that took place in the continental United States, the public office holders from Hawaii and their elections were not included, which only left a couple of incumbent congressmen with Asian heritage from California (Michael M. Honda and Robert T. Matsui) and one from Virginia (Robert C. Scott) excluded from our interview project.

It was admittedly challenging to get ahold of politicians, who often have hectic schedules and are constantly on the road, and it also was difficult to provide a strong incentive for them to cooperate with us in our research. But here is the list of candidates or campaigns we were able to include in this chapter: Two Republicans (Fong and Jindal) and two Democrats (Locke and Wu). Of the four candidates, Jindal is the only one from the South; the rest are from the West Coast. Despite the limitation of sample, this series of interviews did comply with the concepts of theoretical sampling (Strauss & Corbin, 1998) to "maximize opportunities to compare events, incidents, or happenings to determine how a category varies in terms of its properties and dimensions" (p. 202). Therefore, this pool of somewhat diverse interviewees should enable the researchers to bring about the greatest return in the areas of "race factor," "media relation," "campaign issues," "funding source," and "context."

The points extracted from the series of interviews were grouped under the five categories and presented below. The ideas and concepts under these categories were derived from the evidence grounded in the real-life experiences of people involved in campaigns that involved Asian American office seekers. The author of this chapter read the notes and transcripts of these interviews and induced the concepts with the traditional qualitative method (see Charmaz, 1983; Corbin & Strauss, 1998; Glaser & Strauss, 1967, for details) that share common characteristics among these races. In particular, a focused coding method was utilized to identify commonalities and contrasts in the process and features of the campaigns the author observed via the interviews and relevant media coverage.

One of the strengths of interview as a data-collection technique is the possibility that new perspectives can be revealed. The authors in this type of the research were primarily interested in discovering unexplored dimensions and attitudes from the campaign veterans, rather than aiming at generalizing findings as in studies that are more quantitatively oriented. Given this aim, the number of interviews does not necessarily need to be large. It is not uncommon for the sample size of interview project to be small; as one previous study pointed out, "for some projects eight respondents will be perfectly sufficient" (McCracken, 1988, p. 17). Also, after conducting a number of interviews, the interviewer felt that a "saturation" effect seemed to be achieved (similar views were repeatedly expressed by different respondents), which often indicates the sample is sufficient.

RACE FACTOR

The Asian American candidates in question, due to their high-profile campaigns and, perhaps, their ethnic background, received a great deal of local, national, or even international media attention. They were all the first Asian American running for governor, congressman, and senator seat in their respective state or district. Their attitudes and strategies regarding their heritage, however, were slightly different. It appears that Democratic candidates Locke and Wu were more upfront and straightforward about their ethnic backgrounds with their voters, whereas Republicans, especially Bobby Jindal, were more reserved or even reluctant to introduce their heritage to their electorate. The candidates' party affiliation and potential supporters could have attributed to this strategic difference. But differences in regions (the South vs. West Coast) or cultures could be even more influential to candidates' attitude toward their ethnic backgrounds. Republican senatorial candidate Matt Fong, who grew up and campaigned in California, said, "being Asian American can be an advantage since his appearance stood out among White candidates; and when you stand out, people take notice" (personal communication, October 20, 2005). There is a substantial segment of the population on the West Coast that is Asian American; historically and politically, West Coast Americans are more liberal and accepting of things Asian. This is not the case for the South or the Midwest, where Asian American populations are small and there has not been a strong connection of both regions with Asian culture.

When asked whether their ethnic background played any role in their campaigns, the three candidates from the West Coast all said little. David Wu had a typical response:

> Ethnicity in one sense matters and in another sense it does not. By and large, it does not in the following sense: I know that some people will hold my ethnicity against me but probably an equal number view my ethnicity favorably. I think I am just fortunate. I happen to serve an electorate which by and large is neutral. So at the fringes, yea, maybe it matters to a few but they kind of neutralize each other so the overall answer is it does not matter. (D. Wu, personal communication, April 30, 2003)

Their race and ethnicity, unlike the African American or Hispanic counterparts, were not part of their campaign arsenal. It is perfectly understandable, and perhaps crucial, for Asian American candidates to remain "neutral," "mainstream," or "crossover" in major campaigns (Lai, Cho, Kim, & Takeda, 2001) because it is never the case in the continental United States (except for Hawaii, a state with an Asian American majority) that Asian American candidates can rely exclusively on voters of the same ethnic group like African American or Latino candidates do. As Lai and his colleagues pointed out, Asian American elected officials on the U.S. mainland primarily emerge from political districts where Asian Americans make up much less than 50% of the population. They always need to reach out and gain support from various Asian ethnic groups and much more. From the races we examined, it is clear that Asian Americans have steep uphill battles to be elected to public offices at the statewide level.

Given the essential need to have broad appeal among voters, it was interesting to learn that, at the outset of Jindal's primary campaign, he adopted an approach that his campaign messages were sent via conservative radio stations across the state. This tactic was meant to target the Republican stronghold without the unpredictable, unwanted impact of Jindal's Asian Indian image. Jindal avoided personal exposure for so long that even in the end many Louisiana voters still had no idea of Jindal's ethnic background (C. Frink, personal communication, November 18, 2003). Given his Anglo-sounding last name and adopted nickname, Bobby, few Louisianans had a second thought about the background of the new Republican contender in the beginning. But this strategy only worked up to a point.

Only during the run-off election did news media—particularly national media—unveil more of Jindal's ethnic background. This subdued coverage about Jindal's heritage was probably the reason that rumors circulated in parts of Louisiana that he could be a Middle Easterner, according to Baton Rouge *Advocate* reporter, Chris Frink, who covered the election. Being misidentified by Louisiana voters as a Middle Easterner, in an election held only two years after the 9/11, certainly did not produce a result to Jindal's favor. Because he was campaigning in a state where Asian Americans are few and the electorate in general is more conservative than in other parts of the union, Jindal wanted to adopt a nonracial campaign tactic to present his campaign platform in a way that would resonate better with conservative Louisiana residents. Had he focused on his ethnicity or personality, he might have been cast as an outsider. The latter approach could do him no good in the South, where social connections sometimes count more than political commitments and ideals. He portrayed himself as a problem solver and stressed his sterling record in public service, including his prior positions as the president of the University of Louisiana system and Assistant Secretary of the Department of Health and Human Services under the George W. Bush administration. After his success in defeating the other Republican candidate during the primary, he was quoted as saying, "It's not about black, white or yellow. It's about red, white and blue. We're all Americans" (Welch, 2003). This idealist or naive view on race in politics is intriguing, but perhaps necessary in a situation like his.

As Jindal's campaign for governor in 2003 wound down in the run-off, however, Jindal's downplayed ethnicity ironically came back to haunt him in a surprising way. Jindal's campaigner, Luke Letlow, said Democratic gubernatorial contender, Kathleen Blanco, a Cajun Catholic, darkened Jindal's skin tone in one of her attack ads entitled "Wake Up Louisiana" that depicted Jindal as a policy wonk who made heartless cuts to education and health care, two specialized areas Jindal boasted of in his campaign (L. Letlow, personal communication, March 24, 2005). In another instance, Letlow said, a comment made by Blanco's campaign team referenced Louisiana as being "out-Catholiced" by a Hindu (although Jindal and his wife had converted to Catholicism years ago).

It is interesting to point out that Jindal, his campaign team, and the press did not talk about Jindal as an Asian American candidate. Jindal's campaign described him as an Indian American while the local papers labeled him as "non-White." These could be just different choices of term, but seem to show a lack of clear sense of Asian American group identity in Jindal's campaign or the news media. Also, the media did not treat this racial group as seriously or consistently as Latinos or African Americans—rarely did news analysis during elections mention the voting block of Asian Americans. Despite reluctance to admit the influence of race on the part of the candidate and the general public, in the end, political pundits and observers maintained that Jindal's race attributed to his loss to Blanco (e.g., DeBerry, 2003). A poignant finding is that, even with a substantial lead in the last polling result, this staunchly conservative candidate did poorly in the more conservative half of the state—the northern part of Louisiana and the suburbs of New Orleans. Jindal did not win the White voters who traditionally sent Republican candidates to the governor's mansion. Another intriguing result is that Jindal failed to get sufficient Black votes to offset his loss in the "Bubba votes"—individuals who often cast their vote on racial lines.

Both Gary Locke and David Wu indicated that race played a neutral role in their campaigns. Locke was keenly aware of the conservative tendency of the electorate in the eastern part of Washington state. It would be hard for any liberal candidate to win outside of King County (where Seattle is located), and it would be particularly hard for an Asian liberal candidate to muster support from a more rural part of the state. Locke's campaign team adopted a tactic that placed him in the frame of the "Great American Dream" by focusing on his family's immigrant background and achievements and at the same time took a moderate stance on issues. Locke's political consultant, Blair Butterworth, said, "We wanted to be sure that no one was surprised when they learned that Gary was an Asian American. We didn't want any sticker shock" (B. Butterworth, personal communication, March 24, 2003). Interestingly, they also capitalized on the clichéd stereotypes about Asians and Asian Americans who live in the United States—that they are hardworking, exceedingly educated, and family oriented—and used these themes and Gary Locke's personal stories in their TV ads. By featuring these positive stereotypes, they were able to appeal to the majority of families and also feed journalists with lots of story lines.

Gary Locke's out-in-the-open tactic suited him just right, but might not work in every state of the union. Even Oregon, just south of Washington, does not have a comparable percentage of Asian American population, nor does it have the right atmosphere to embrace and emphasize a candidate's minority background in campaigns. David Wu, the current congressman representing Oregon's first district, explained that there were conflicting forces from various ethnic groups or individuals in his district, but they seemed to cancel each other out in the end. David Wu's campaign aide Jeston Black said that Wu's ethnicity has never been an issue in the 2002 campaign, insisting that it has never been considered a hindrance or a benefit in any way. Wu recognized that there will never be a majority minority district for Asian American candidates, so it is extremely important for Asian American candidates to "build bridges, find the commonality, and just get on the same wavelength with other people" (D. Wu, personal communication, April 30, 2003).

Even in California, where Asian Americans make up almost 10% of its total population, Asian American candidates seemed to tread carefully on the heritage line, hoping to avoid invoking historical distrust between ethnicities and races in California while attracting as much—or more—non-Asian as well as Asian Americans' support. After all, it is imperative for any Asian American candidate to draw substantial numbers of *all* voters to their camp, particularly in statewide races when votes from certain ethnic pockets are simply insufficient. As David Wu pointed out in the interview, Matt Fong witnessed conflicting, complicated, and assorted entrenched interests from different ethnic groups in California, a finding that is echoed in an article by Geron, de la Cruz, Saito, and Singh (2001). Based on Lien, Conway, and Wong's (2004) landmark survey of Asian Americans across the nation, the *Asian American* panethnic label was accepted by only 15% of the surveyed Asian Americans; most respondents preferred an ethnic-based identity, such as *Filipino American* or *Vietnamese American*. Fong failed to gain pan-Asian American support in his bid for the Senate seat; disappointingly, he was able to garner endorsements from Korean and Chinese communities, but got the cold shoulder from Japanese, Filipino, and other Asian American opinion leaders. The reason for the mixed support for Fong from Asian American communities could be embedded in different party affiliations, issue stances, and prior interethnic interactions. But he said that it is understandable, and perhaps reasonable, that Asian Americans, just like average Americans, put certain issues ahead of ethnic linkage during elections. This could be a major difference between Asian American voters and Black and Latino counterparts and might well be the reason that Asian Americans were rarely discussed in the news media and campaign literature as being a voting block.

MEDIA RELATIONS

Based on our content analysis study of the press coverage of the five races (for details, see chap. 4, this volume), the media seemed to devote a fair share of space and time to covering Asian American candidates and their opponents. Overall, in terms of valence of the campaign news, it also appeared that candidates of opposite camps were covered rather evenly. Both Gary Locke and David Wu were by and large contented with the coverage of their respective campaigns and succeeded in obtaining editorial endorsements from both the Seattle *Times* and the *Oregonian*, the major newspapers in both regions. One surprising finding yielded from the two interviews is that they endeavored to play their ethnicity to their advantage with a rather unusual and fascinating tactic. Due to the rarity of having an Asian American candidate competing for high-level public offices, they said they immediately stood out and appeared to easily get both the media and the voters interested in them. Moreover, Locke's campaign consultant, Butterworth, pointed to a preemptive strategy that incorporated race and existing Asian stereotypes that simply worked to Locke's favor. He said,

> Because you know the first time you go around on a campaign the papers have to cover you. So they were out there in a positive way reporting our theme of the Great American Dream. Well, when you put your ethnicity in that framework, it's very very hard for anyone to deal with it in any kind of negative way, a sort of immunity to attacks. (B. Butterworth, personal communication, March 24, 2003)

Apparently the Locke team was pleased with the result of their straightforward strategy with the media and the general public. Perhaps their strategy really did work. To a certain extent, David Wu also was open with the media on his ethnic roots and activities—he let voters know he worked with the Asian American caucus in the past, but he did not go all out as Locke did by using family stories in TV ads. Both Locke and Wu won their races, so they probably did not care that much about the fine details of media coverage. Based on our qualitative analysis, however, it is clear that the content of both campaigns still included subtly negative, stereotypical images that could have tipped the journalistic balance. Locke and Wu did not address the difference of coverage between local and national papers. Perhaps due to the geographic location of Jindal's campaign, Louisiana, Letlow contended that the national press seemed to play up the race issue, whereas the local press did not mention the race factor as much. This point is echoed by Chris Frink, the *Advocate* reporter. He felt that the local press felt uncomfortable about bringing up the race factor in their campaign coverage, whereas the national press had leeway to highlight it because it did not need to worry too much about stirring up the reaction of local readers. By the end of the 2003 gubernatorial campaign, however, major Louisiana papers had all endorsed Jindal in their editorials.

Matt Fong seemed to be more willing than other interviewees to express his feelings about the press and provided tips for future Asian American political hopefuls. He indicated that he had experienced more up-close and personal confrontation with the media on his campaign trail. His critique of media bias resides not only in the political spectrum, but also in the racial domain. He, like many Republicans and conservative constituents, voiced his concern over the media's liberal bias. For the latter category, he particularly recounted two despicable instances—one in San Francisco and the other in San Diego—where reporters deliberately asked him which side he would pick if China and the United States were to have a conflict. He said he would not have been irritated if all candidates had been asked this type of question; for example, his Democratic opponent, Barbara Boxer, could have been asked about her loyalty to Israel versus the United States. In the interview, he expressed deep disgust toward the media's racist treatment of his senatorial campaign, which occurred despite the fact that he had been in public service for a long time and his background—a fourth-generation Chinese American and Lieutenant Colonel in the U.S. Air Force Reserve—was well known to the press. Additionally, he argued that Al Gore's fundraising scandal in Asian American communities in California, which was covered thoroughly in the press, affected him greatly. Many affluent Chinese Americans told him in person that they were not willing to donate money to his campaign because they did not want the IRS to investigate them. Those potential funding sources did not want their names printed in the newspapers, and they advised Fong to hold off on fundraising activities in their communities until the scandal faded away. To him, the media and Washington's treatments of Asian Americans' donation to political entities were biased and smacked of racism.

Fong also attributed his failure to unseat Boxer in 1996 to unpolished communication skills. He expressed the view that Asian Americans in general value deeds more than words and do not necessarily recognize the importance and impact of media communication. He lamented that, although he was a successful banker, lawyer, and engineer, he did not learn how to stand up and make a resonating, passionate speech. He said, "I was studious and focused on the substance. If there is any lesson I drew from my failed bid it is when you get into a high-profile campaign in a media stage you do need to learn how to communicate to the media" (M. Fong, personal communication, October 20, 2005). In addition to skills in media and speech, he also advocated that all candidates for office should have stage experience and know how to perform in front of audiences and cameras. It is advice rarely given by political veterans, but from the perspective of communication-centered politics, it is vitally valuable and rings true. A great number of successful politicians are indeed originally from Hollywood and candidates' appearance, manners, and verbal and nonverbal presentation do affect voters' perceptions greatly. A recent study (Todorov, Mandisodza, Goren, & Hall, 2005) even showed that people's unreflective inferences of competence—based solely on candidates' facial appearance—can predict the outcomes of elections.

CAMPAIGN ISSUES

Despite the differences in party line, the offices they ran for, and geo-graphic region of these races, all of the Asian American candidates interviewed focused exclusively on a small number of issues, particularly education. Primarily because the American public seems to associate Asian Americans with high education, work ethics, and devotion to professionalism, Asian American candidates love to concentrate on this issue. As a result, it is natural for these Asian American candidates to capitalize on the fixed stereotype. Moreover, education appeared to be a safe bet for Asian American candidates. For Gary Locke, education is sort of a personal calling because he strongly feels that education is the best way for any person to move out of hardship and enter mainstream America. The issue was well woven into his major campaign theme of the Great American Dream. Education also was the number one issue that David Wu emphasized in his bid for Congress. Coincidently, it was not only Wu's favorite issue, but also the favorite issue with Oregon voters. Black, Wu's political consultant, said that various polls showed that education continued to be foremost in the minds of voters. Wu said that the issue of education was later turned into a test for candidates' consistency and commitment toward public education in the first district of Oregon. For Bobby Jindal, education was a natural choice because he had been president of the University of Louisiana System under governor Mike Foster before he moved to Washington to serve under the Bush administration. His platform in education dovetailed neatly with Bush's policy, which advocated systematic tests and school vouchers.

Democratic candidates Locke and Wu wanted their appeal among voters to be broad and therefore addressed the issues that moderate Republicans care about. Therefore, they also initiated platforms in tradi-tionally Republican turf such as crime and business development. Locke addressed the importance of keeping the community safe by launching one TV ad that featured his own father, who was once robbed and shot in his store. At the end of the ad, Locke adroitly delivered the image of being tough on crime, which, according to Butterworth, "made the Locke campaign come out of the gate." Likewise, to attract African Americans in Louisiana, Jindal, the Republican gubernatorial candidate who embraced hard-core conservative stances on abortion, tax cuts, and gun control, also addressed civil rights and succeeded in gaining endorsements from heavyweight Black leaders, including New Orleans mayor Ray Nagin.

If only candidates were all so lucky as to be able to concentrate on the issues they personally are passionate about. Jindal's political appointments in health care, both in state government and under the Bush administration, earned him harsh critiques from his opponent. Matt Fong said he was actually more interested in tax reform and international affairs, especially the relationship between the United States and the up-and-coming economies of the Pacific Rim region. Back then he had expressed the belief that the United States would have closer and possibly more tense relationships with Asian countries in the 21st century and that too few representatives in the Congress had the cultural background and required knowledge to handle these relationships well and right. But unfortunately, he said, few Californians would be interested in that issue, and instead he had to focus on health care, environment, and abortion. Based on the results of this study, one can easily see that there are no specific issues focused on by all Asian American candidates. But education appears to be the single issue that Asian American candidates felt strongly about and emphasized in their campaigns.

FUNDING

In the current U.S. electoral system, sufficient funding is crucial to success in all races. The first thing Fong remembered during his interview was the high cost of his campaign. It cost him $2 million a week to broadcast one commercial across California. He also said that his incumbent opponent got high-voltage stars like Barbra Streisand to gain support from wealthy individuals and eventually out-spent him in that campaign. The Asian American candidates interviewed in this study indicated that individual donations are the main staple of their campaign funding. They were less successful in garnering professional, corporate, or industry support. They were all enthusiastic, yet cautious, of raising money in various Asian American communities and associations. On the one hand, they felt those citizens who shared similar ethnic backgrounds with them would be more supportive and understanding of their political aspiration; on the other hand, they were apprehensive of potential illegal contributions made by non-naturalized Asians. They were all acutely aware of John Huang and Charlie Trie, who were accused of raising foreign money and funneling it to Al Gore's presidential campaign coffers. Receiving illegal donations would not only be a breach of campaign laws, but could lead to defeat through deadly publicity.

It is interesting to find that having an Asian American in the races seemed to elevate the chance for Asian American voters—even from other parts of the country—to donate. Due to various historic and cultural factors, Asian Americans have been described as politically apathetic in the U.S. political arena, but with their economic ascent, they seem to be more likely to exert their influence on politics with their newly formed monetary muscle. Matt Fong observed the lack of Asian votes in the 1960s and 1970s when his legendary mother, March Fong Eu, ran for public offices in California. He noticed a dramatic difference since the 1990s. He said, "a lot of Asian Americans are successful business people, entrepreneurs, and they have the ability to give, which exceeds their number. Their dollar power is stronger than their voting power" (M. Fong, personal communication, October 20, 2005).

One significant finding from this study that supports the Lai et al. (2001) earlier observation of Asian American political participation is that these Asian American office-seekers were not able to attract support—voting or financial—from the broader Asian American population. Jindal was reported to have received substantial funding from wealthy Indian Americans across the nation, but did not get much donation from another significant Asian American ethnic group in Louisiana, the Vietnamese. Fong also reported a similar scenario—he received financial backing from various Chinese American and Korean American communities and civic organizations in California, but failed to get formal endorsements from Japanese American leaders. Based on these findings, one would conclude that Asian American candidates will need to diversify their funding sources and attract endorsement from interest groups whose goals are in line with their campaign platforms.

CONTEXT

It is perhaps useful to discuss the context of the races in which the Asian American candidates were running because the situational factors could be more important than any other determinants we have discussed so far. Except for Jindal, Asian Americans seemed to run as moderates in the races, and they fared much better when they faced extremely right or left candidates. It certainly was the case for Gary Locke in his first gubernatorial campaign. He got off to a good start with a big crowd of liberals in the primary and faced an ultraconservative Republican opponent, Ellen Craswell, in the run-off. It was, once again, the case in 2000 when Locke ran for reelection against John Carlson, a conservative former radio host. Somehow, candidates need auspicious situations to win elections. This is precisely why Locke's consultant commented, "Gary is not only good but he is also lucky" (B. Butterworth, personal communication, March 24, 2003).

Good luck can carry a candidate a long way. David Wu also described the favorable situation for him to win in his first congressional race. In the 1998 race, Molly Bordonaro was considered a strong candidate, and she scared off quite a few moderate candidates. Wu said that Bordonaro probably would have won the election if another moderate candidate joined the race and took the votes that would go to him. Wu was probably being modest, but when asked what worked for him in his campaigns, he said, "I have thought about this question for a while and quite frankly I have no idea how we won" (D. Wu, personal communication, April 30, 2003). Wu's candid reply vividly shows the complexity of running effective political campaigns and the many unknown factors that can be constantly at work in the election process.

Running against incumbents is known to be extremely difficult. Matt Fong faced a tough opponent with a strong track record on certain issues and great financial resources to sway voters' perceptions. Fong expressed regret at not being more aggressive in his campaign—attacking an incumbent female senator was apparently not his cup of tea. Jindal faced a somewhat similar situation in his gubernatorial bid against Kathleen Blanco, who, arguably, cunningly made an informal deal with him not to run a negative campaign and subsequently broke the promise. But Jindal never fought back. Political pundits unanimously said this could be the fatal blow (Gill, 2003a, 2003b). In this Louisiana race, both Blanco and Jindal are conservative candidates—regardless of their different party affiliations—so the real choice for voters was not based on the candidates' issue stances, but on history and connection with the community and, perhaps, the candidate's skin color (DeBerry, 2003).

LIMITATIONS

This chapter has aimed at collecting and organizing thoughts generated from a series of interviews with Asian American candidates, their consultants, and one journalist who participated in the political campaigns analyzed in this book. Their viewpoints were juxtaposed with findings of other election studies. The results presented in this chapter have shed light on the campaign scenes that few people had observed first hand. Readers of this chapter should be reminded that some factors may have influenced our results. All the interviews were conducted by the first author of this book. It was likely that the first author's own Asian American background could have affected the respondents' answers. For example, several interviewees assumed that the only purpose of the interview was intended to talk about the race/ethnicity of the candidates in those campaigns. The first author had to explain that race/ethnicity was one of our interest areas, but it was certainly not the *only* issue we would like to discuss with them. The first author also had to explain to the interviewees that the content of the conversations would not be shared with their local media or their opponents' camps and that the interview recording would be used for the proposed book only. In a number of instances, it was obvious that some interviewees felt a little awkward talking about the race factor and immediately gave safe, socially acceptable responses. The first author did his best to solicit honest, and even politically incorrect, answers from the campaign veterans. We hope that the information presented in this chapter sheds some qualitative light on the campaigns we have studied.

REFERENCES

Charmaz, K. (1983). The grounded theory method: An explication and interpretation. In R. Emerson (Ed.), *Contemporary field research* (pp. 109–126). Boston: Little, Brown.

Corbin, J., & Strauss, A. (1998). *Basics of qualitative research: Techniques and procedures for developing grounded theory.* Thousand Oaks, CA: Sage.

DeBerry, J. (2003, November 21). How race colors voting decisions. *The* (New Orleans, LA) *Times-Picayune,* Metro, p. 7.

Geron, K., de la Cruz, E., Saito, L. T., & Singh, J. (2001). Asian Pacific Americans' social movements and interest groups. *PSOnline,* pp. 619–624.

Gill, J. (2003a, November 19). Jindal's silence was golden—for Blanco. The *Times-Picayune,* Metro, p. 7.

Gill, J. (2003b, December 3). Questions linger about racism in election. The *Times-Picayune,* Metro, p 7.

Glaser, B., & Strauss, A. (1967). *Discovery of grounded theory.* Chicago: Aldine.

Lai, J. S., Cho, W. K. T., Kim, T. P., & Takeda, O. (2001). Asian Pacific-American campaigns, elections, and elected officials. *PSOnline,* pp. 611–617.

Lien, P. T., Conway, M. M., & Wong, J. (2004). *The politics of Asian Americans: Diversity & community.* New York: Routledge.

McCracken, G. (1988). *The long interview.* Newbury Park, CA: Sage.

Todorov, A., Mandisodza, A. N., Goren, A., & Hall, C. C. (2005). Inferences of competence from faces predict election outcomes. *Science, 308,* 1623–1626.

Welch, W. (2003, November 10). Polls suggest a volatile governor's race in La. *USA Today,* p. 13A.

Chapter 7

Perception of Political Candidates' Electability: Examining the Impact of Gender and Race

Voters' perception is crucial to the success of anyone seeking public offices of all levels. We set out to study this subject because we wonder how Asian American candidates are perceived, compared to candidates of different ethnic backgrounds. In the 2004 Democratic presidential primary, Howard Dean—although widely supported and leading in the polls for a substantial period of time—made the notorious shout in Iowa that was broadcast and relayed repeatedly. Partially because of this incident, he was perceived as being less likely to beat the incumbent, George W. Bush, in the presidential election (Brooks, 2004). From that time forward, Dean was overshadowed by another Democratic candidate, John Kerry, who appeared to be more moderate and conventional, and thus more electable (Shaw, 2004). The *Economist* reported that "Kerry's perceived ability to beat George Bush—that magical aura of electability—has gone from being an important advantage to the decisive one" ("He's Got a Ticket to Ride," 2004). Democrats would rather choose a less divisive candidate to beat the incumbent than to pick a candidate popular inside their party who would be less electable across the nation. To many political observers, the electorate's assessment of whether a candidate is electable determines how one votes in the election and is, perhaps, more crucial than the candidate's platforms. Therefore, *electability* became the buzzword in the 2004 campaign circle and seems to merit a more serious look (Calmes, 2007; Meyrowitz, 1992; Welch & Studlar, 1996).

Perception of electability not only shifts across candidates' political platforms, but also among their innate attributes—demographics (Calmes, 2007; Meyrowitz, 1992; Welch & Studlar, 1996). Although gender and

119

race have been studied in a wide range of fields of social sciences, little research has systematically investigated the combined impact of both gender *and* race—beyond Blacks and Whites—of political candidates on election results, as well as how perceived electability is intertwined with gender and race. Recent census data indicate that more and more Americans are non-Whites; moreover, given that more females have actively participated in public affairs and run for public offices since the mid-20th century, it is important to investigate whether women's ultimate realization of political participation—holding public offices—has been truly equal and fair.

Given the unlikelihood of having candidates of all kinds of demographic backgrounds in the same race, this study resorts to a test of hypothetic setting by conducting a 2 × 4 experiment that used diverse adult subjects to evaluate congressional candidates of different gender and races with identical credentials, issue stances, and political experience. This research aims to explore the impact of the perceived candidate attributes derived from gender and races on people's voting decision and assessment of their electability.

Because this experimental research examines whether a candidate's gender and race influence support from potential voters, this research can serve as a benchmark that measures the overall attitudes toward races and gender roles of public office holders among Americans at the beginning of the 21st century. Future research that focuses on candidates' demographic backgrounds could therefore be compared with the findings of this study. In addition, several key variables that might influence voters' perception, including participants' experience of interaction with other races, their attitude toward equality in the society, and media usage, were taken into account in this study. The design of this study is likely the first to systematically examine the relationship between race and gender and candidate assessment.

ATTITUDES TOWARD RACE AND GENDER IN THE UNITED STATES

Most studies on racial attitudes in the United States focus on White Americans' attitudes toward African Americans (e.g., Entman & Rojecki, 2000; Peffley & Hurwitz, 1998; Rada, 2000; Schuman, Steeh, Bobo, & Krysan, 1997; Tuch & Martin, 1997). It appears that contemporary racism has gradually replaced blatant discrimination in the United States (Entman, 1990, 1994). Whites have become more likely to believe—or at least to voice publicly—that African Americans are equal and should be treated equally in the society. In recent years, a larger number of African Americans have been elected to state or federal offices, indicating some progress in political involvement. Nevertheless, it is too early to proclaim the end of racism because those who still harbor racist thoughts often resort to more disguised, subtle, and indirect ways of expressing it (Dovidio, Gaertner, Nier, Kawakami, & Hodson, 2004; Sniderman, Piazza, Tetlock, & Kendrick, 1991). For instance, in a recent study, fictional applicants with White-sounding names are significantly more likely than those with Black-sounding names to receive an invitation for job interviews (Bertrand & Mullainathan, 2004).

In recent years, Latino Americans have gained more political clout with increasing population in the United States (Affigne, 2000). Latinos are the largest racial/ethnic minority group in the United States, and their growth rate, surpassing all other ethnic groups in the country, will remain high in the future (U.S. Census Bureau, 2005). Evidence of Latino power was showcased in the August 22, 2005, issue of *TIME* magazine, which published a cover story on prominent Latino figures in the United States, entitled "The 25 Most Influential Hispanics in America." Not only were more Latinos sent to Washington in the last decade, but the Latino voting bloc has gained a great deal of notice across the political spectrum.

In sharp contrast, Asian Americans are not considered to have much political clout partially because, regardless of their citizenship, they have often been perceived as aliens or outsiders in the United States (Larson, 2006; R. Lee, 1999; F. Wu, 2002; Yee, 1992). For instance, during World War II, Japanese Americans were sent to internment camps because their "mother country" was at war with the United States, although their German or Italian American counterparts did not receive the same treatment (Tung, 1974; J. Wu & Song, 2000). The perpetual sojourner image prevails until today. Matt Fong, a fourth-generation Chinese American who ran for a Senate seat against Barbara Boxer in 1998, was repeatedly asked about the issue of national loyalty in his campaign trail. David Wu, a congressman of Oregon, even with his official pass, was barred from entering the U.S. Department of Energy building by security guards who did not believe he looked like an American (Barnett, 2001). According to a recent nationwide survey, 25% of Americans interviewed hold strong negative views toward Chinese Americans, 23% of Americans would not want a Chinese American to be the president, and 7% would not work for an Asian American CEO (Anti-Defamation League, 2001).

Racial attitude is normally measured by scale of opposite adjectives, such as *violent* versus *peaceful*, *hardworking* versus *lazy*, and *responsible* versus *irresponsible,* or by descriptive statements such as "African Americans are intellectually bright" and "Asian Americans are buying up too much land in the United States" (Ho & Jackson, 2001; Sniderman & Carmines, 1997). Although Americans' attitudes toward Asian Americans are generally negative, at least they can be straightforward. When it comes to African Americans, participants seem less willing to voice their honest opinion, which reflects a sensitized, politicized mechanism of public opinion. Researchers had to use alterative measures to tease out Whites' true attitudes toward Blacks (Sniderman, Brody, & Tetlock, 1991; Sniderman & Carmines, 1997). In a method called the Excuse Experiment, researchers created a situation in which White participants "who say they think well of blacks are deliberately given a socially acceptable excuse to make a negative judgment of blacks, precisely in order to see if they take advantage of it" (Sniderman & Carmines, 1997, p. 13). An example is, using a 2 (White vs. Black) × 2 (high school graduates vs. dropouts) design about a mother on welfare, subjects were asked whether they think this welfare mother is likely to make an honest effort to exit welfare the following year (Sniderman & Carmines, 1997). This study found that those who spoke well about Blacks sincerely meant it because the subjects did not take advantage of socially acceptable excuses. Nevertheless, a substantial number of respondents were found to express negative feelings toward Blacks, saying they are violent, lazy, and irresponsible.

Partially due to the feminist movement and legal protections, blatant discrimination against women in the workplace and other social arenas has become less common. Nevertheless, achieving complete gender equality in U.S. society still has a long way to go. For instance, women consistently earn a lower wage than men at a roughly .75 ratio (Bernstein, 2004). There is also a "glass ceiling" and a wide gender gap—in terms of both numbers and salaries—among top executive positions in corporate America (Bertrand & Hallock, 2001). In the political arena, female office holders are still outnumbered by men. The number of women in the U.S. Congress, for example, still lags far behind the percentage of their population. People's entrenched attitudes about women's roles could be at work.

One can attribute the efforts of promoting diversity in U.S. society to the improved relationships between races and gender. The logic behind such efforts is the prior contact hypothesis. Essentially, this hypothesis posits that contacts with people of different racial backgrounds can alleviate negative stereotypes of the groups and, therefore, foster positive or normal attitudes toward each other (Allport, 1954; Amir, 1969; Fujioka, 1999; Pettigrew, 1998; Tan, Fujioka, & Lucht, 1997). Although diversity has not been focused on in the literature of political representation, it is reasonable and logical to link prior contact as a factor in the perception of candidates' electability. Therefore, variables testing formal and informal contacts with various races are included in this study.

COMMUNICATION THEORIES
AND RACIAL AND GENDER ATTITUDES

Three bodies of knowledge in communication contribute to the theoretical framework of this study are (a) cultivation analysis, (b) uses and gratifications (U&G), and (c) third-person effect.

First, cultivation analysis theorizes that heavy TV use may lead to believing in the reality constructed by the media industry (Gerbner, Gross, Jackson-Beeck, Jeffries-Fox, & Signorielli, 1978; Gerbner, Gross, Morgan, & Signorielli, 1980; Gerbner, Gross, Signorielli, Morgan, & Jackson-Beeck, 1979). Due to the constant representation of violence on the TV screen, heavy viewers may perceive the world as mean and scary. These audiences tend to overestimate the chance of being victimized and the number of people involved in law enforcement and crimes. These viewers also are more likely to consider their fellow citizens untrustworthy. Although most cultivation literature focuses on TV viewing, other media were found to cultivate as effectively as TV (Signorielli & Morgan, 1990).

Cultivation theory, at least in the earlier versions, assumes that the audiences are passively influenced by media content. The U&G approach, however, presents an opposite view. Technically, U&G is more of a research perspective than a solid communication theory. U&G aims to explain why, how, where, and when people consume specific media to meet their needs and wants. Specific social and psychological needs or motives of audience members help determine their media consumption (Blumler & Katz, 1974; Rubin & Perse, 1987; Severin & Tankard, 1997). For instance, teenagers who are sensation-seeking, aggressive, and alienated are attracted to violent films, websites, and computer content (Slater, 2003).

The insights from both theoretical approaches helped establish a connection between media consumption and attitudes toward different races and genders. Communication scholars have long argued that negative media portrayals of racial minorities contribute to discrimination against these groups. At the same time, women are often portrayed as being inferior (e.g., passive, less intelligent) to men and as exploitable sex objects, especially in advertising. Such negative depictions of women can lead to lower evaluation, discrimination, or even violence against women (Cortese, 2004; Goffman, 1976; Kilbourne, 1999; T. Lee & Hwang, 2002; Meyers, 1999).

Negative, stereotypical portrayals of minority groups are still common in the mainstream media in the United States (Lester, 1996). Entman and Rojecki (2000) reported that both news and entertainment media constructed African Americans as inferior in many ways, which helped shape or reinforce Euro-Americans' ambivalent attitudes toward them. A content analysis by Dixon and Linz (2000) revealed that Blacks and Latinos are overrepresented as law-breakers on TV news. J. Lee (1994) discovered the largest number of news stories on Asian Americans were reported in connection to illegal immigration, crime, and gang violence. Hamamoto (1994) and R. Lee (1999) argued that the media tend to portray Asians and Asian Americans as aliens or outsiders who could never become part of the mainstream America. Valentino (1999) reported the news media's ability to activate racial attitudes via stereotypic portrayals of minorities, which subsequently affect voters' evaluations of political candidates.

Busselle and Crandall (2002) found that only a few studies have investigated the true linkage between media exposure and perception toward minorities, but the unveiled linkage seems solid. For instance, a higher level of attention to news on race relations may lead to a perception that greater socioeconomic disparities exist between White and African Americans. Such attention also is positively related to the belief that such difference is likely due to discrimination and lack of job opportunities (Gandy & Baron, 1992). Viewing entertainment programs on TV was found to be associated with the belief that Blacks are more successful than Whites, but news viewing was found to contribute to the contrary perception (Armstrong, Neuendorf, & Brentar, 1992). In an experiment, participants were more likely to judge that a Black perpetrator in a news story was "lazy" and had a "lack of intelligence" compared with a White perpetrator (Gilliam & Iyengar, 1998).

In addition, Busselle and Crandall (2002) found that watching different genres of TV programs (drama, sitcom, and news) influences respondents' estimates of the income and education of White and African Americans, as well as possible reasons behind such achievements. News viewing is positively related to the belief that lack of motivation results in socioeconomic differences between Blacks and Whites. Watching sitcoms is positively related to the education and income level of African Americans. TV drama viewing predicts the perception that Whites are better educated than African Americans (Busselle & Crandall, 2002). Because of the linkage between media consumption and racial attitudes, the questionnaire of the present study included a number of media use variables.

The third group of communication literature that led to the present study is the third-person effect theory. Since Davidson's (1983) seminal study, dozens of articles have been written on this subject (Perloff, 1993, 1999). Essentially, this theory argues that people tend to believe that media content would have a stronger effect on others (third person) than on themselves. We extrapolated from the theory that one would overestimate his own political openness and assume others to be more sexist or racist when assessing diverse candidates. Insights from the Excuse Experiment mentioned above and the third-person effect theory helped us measure potential voters' racial attitudes in terms of how likely they would vote for a candidate who is either female or a member of a racial minority, or both.

Although the Excuse Experiments by Sniderman and colleagues (1991, 1997) reported that their participants proved sincere about their feelings toward Blacks, modern racism literature (e.g., Dovidio et al., 2004; Entman, 1990, 1994; Sniderman, Brody, et al., 1991; Sniderman, Piazza, et al., 1991) still suggests that many citizens are reluctant to express their true racial attitudes. Therefore, asking whether a participant would vote for a Black, Asian American, or woman candidate is likely to receive a socially desirable answer. To tease out their true racial and gender attitudes as operationalized by voting for a racial minority and/or female politician, respondents should be asked to estimate how likely others would support such a candidate. Based on the literature reviewed, the following research questions and hypotheses were formed:

RQ1: Do the race and sex of candidates predict participants' perceived electability and voting likelihood?

RQ2: Does participants' belief in equal opportunity predict their assessment of non-White candidates?

In light of the literature on third-person effect, it is reasonable to posit that people tend to portray themselves in a more positive light. Supporting non-White and female candidates is a politically correct and/or socially desirable action, which could result in a discovery of reverse third-person effect or first-person effect. Therefore, we hypothesized that

H1: Participants' assessment of their own voting likelihood for non-White candidates is better than others'.

Literature shows that people's direct or mediated experience with other races may play a role in their judgment of the racial group and, therefore, influence their perception of minority candidate. In light of this rationale, the following hypothesis was formed:

H2: Participants' personal experience with the race of the candidate may predict electability and voting likelihood for non-White candidate.

METHOD

Experimental Design

The present study employed a 4 × 2 experimental design that incorporated four races/ethnicities (White, African, Asian, and Latino Americans) and both sexes (female and male) into the stimuli that participants read. The experiment device consists of a detailed instruction, a pretest, one of the eight stimuli (a congressional candidate's color direct mail) inserted in the middle, and a posttest questionnaire.

All participants in this experiment first received a pretest that aimed to capture their prior political experience, attitude toward gender and races in general, and frequency of contacts with all four races socially and formally (e.g., at work). The stimulus of the experiment is a typical letter-sized, color campaign material (double-sided and printed in quality, glossy paper) that includes a candidate's headshot, short biography, education background, political experience, and issue stances. The four issues covered in the print campaign material are education, health care, economic development, and national security, on all of which the candidate advocated moderate solutions and therefore did not resemble the political platform of a typical Republican or Democratic ticket.

The setting of the race is a congressional (U.S. House of Representatives) seat in Pennsylvania, a considered toss-up state in the 2004 election. The fact that the race is set in Pennsylvania could compel participants to think more about electability. The researchers purposely selected this state, with which participants from the South and Pacific Northwest are less likely to be familiar. The only variation in the stimulus (i.e., the manipulation) is the candidate featured. There are eight candidates rotated as the candidate for the subjects to read about—White male, White female, Latino male, Latina female, Asian male, Asian female, Black male, and Black female. These eight candidates' names and pictures are the only two cues to disclose their gender and race. It is worth noting that the two Latino photos used in the stimuli appear more like White than other races—so their Spanish last names (Sanchez) served as an additional cue. To ensure the photos' homogeneity, aside from their identical photo size, all eight fictional candidates are in their mid-40s, dressed formally, and rated to be in the same level of attractiveness by 30 college students. Analysis of variance (ANOVA) results showed no difference of attractiveness among any of the candidates.

Each participant of the experiment was exposed to only one of the eight candidates who were competing for the congressional seat. After the exposure, participants were asked to assess the likelihood of voting for the candidate under different circumstances and to evaluate the candidate's credibility, competency, and electability on 4-point Likert scales. They also were asked to state how likely they and others would vote for the feature candidate. For example, the specific wording in two items is: "If you were a Pennsylvanian, how likely would *you* vote for this candidate" and "If your friends and family were Pennsylvanians, how likely would *they* vote for this candidate?" In addition, the participants were asked to assess the likelihood that the candidate they read about can be elected under four discrete circumstances. The first scenario is a simple assessment from the participant. The second scenario was described as the feature candidate running against an incompetent incumbent. The third and fourth scenarios included a third White, highly qualified candidate in the race—the only difference between the two scenarios is that the fourth assessment was the likely assessment of participants' friends and family. The manipulation check in the posttest consists of three multiple-choice questions: the sex of the candidate, the office this candidate is running for, and the race/ethnicity of the candidate.

Participants

The participants in the experiment were recruited from the staffs (including a few of their spouses or partners, as well as other family members who are adults) of two public universities. One is located in the South, the other in the Pacific Northwest of the United States. The rationale behind the recruitment strategy is that these two regions are culturally and politically different, with the South leaning toward the Republican Party and the Northwest slightly favoring the Democratic Party. Having subjects from both geographic regions can elevate the level of representation of the sample. Another step the researchers took to ensure a higher validity was to have university staffs rather than college students—mostly more than 20 years old, with more voting experience and a higher age variance—as participants. The practice of having college students as subjects has been criticized repeatedly for concern of validity (Gordon,

Slade, & Schmitt, 1986). It seems particularly important for this project to include participants who have more political experience than undergraduate students. Those who participated in the experiment were given a $5 coupon to a local restaurant or bookstore. About half of the 296 subjects were recruited from the South (n = 143, 48.3%), and the rest came from the northwest region (n = 153, 51.7%) of the United States; 288 participants reported their age, ranging between 19 and 76, with a mean age of 39.34 (SD = 12.23) and median of 40. As for their race, the majority (n = 211, 72%) were White, 47 (16%) were Black, 10 were Latino/Latina (3.4%), 7 were Asian Americans (2.4%), 4 were Native Americans (1.4%), 14 (4.8%) answered "other," and 3 did not indicated their racial background and therefore were coded as "missing."

RESULTS

Our first research question examined the impact of race and gender on candidates' electability and winning assessment. Of the four groups, the White candidates' electability is the highest[1] (M = 1.93, SD = .673), closely followed by the Hispanic candidates (M = 1.96, SD = .711). Asian American (M = 2.22, SD = .763) and African American (M = 2.23, SD = .768) candidates are not perceived as being as electable as the above two ethnic groups. The one-way ANOVA test indicates that the race factor is statistically significant in predicting a candidate's electability (F = 3.57, df = 3, p = .015), although the post-hoc tests (Tukey-HSD and Scheffe) did not show any of the differences among the four groups to be statistically significant at the 5% level. The electability differences between White and African Americans and between White and Asian Americans are significant only at 6.6% and 8.7%, respectively.

As to gender's prediction on a candidate's electability, males (M = 2.00, SD = .697) seem to score slightly better than females (M = 2.17, SD = .772), although the gender difference appears to be on the edge of statistical significance (t = −1.944, df = 293, p = .053). However, it is interesting to point out that when both race and gender of candidates were entered into ANOVA, the gender factor turns out to be statistically significant (F = 4.102, df = 1, p = .044). The interaction term between race and gender, however, is not statistically significant (F = 1.558, df = 3, p = .200).

---

[1]Because the scale used in the measurement device designates 1 as *most likely* and 4 as *least likely*, the smaller the means, the better the likelihood.

As indicated in the "Method" section, subjects were asked to assess the likelihood the candidate they read about can be elected under four discrete circumstances. MANOVA was executed to see whether race and gender might have led to different assessments. The results show that the race factor is a significant predictor (F = 2.288, p = .007, Δ^2 = .032), but gender is not (F = 1.832, p = .123, Δ^2 = .026), nor is the interaction term between gender and race (F = 1.522, p = .111, Δ^2 = .021). Specifically, race is a significant factor predicting winning likelihood in two election scenarios in which there is an incompetent incumbent and a third candidate who is White and equally competent as the candidate featured in the campaign material. One interesting finding is that the race factor affected a participant's own assessment about the feature candidate's electability when there is a third White candidate (F = 3.057, p = .032, η^2 = .031) in the election less than a participant's estimate of others' assessment (F = 6.008, p = .001, Δ^2 = .060), suggesting a third-person effect in the assessments. In other words, other people (third persons) are more likely to be affected by the candidate's race. As to gender effect on winning likelihood assessment, the scenarios in which gender led to different assessments are those when the opponent in the race is an incumbent (F = 4.969, p = .027 Δ^2 = .017) and when there is a third White candidate in the race (F = 4.969, p = .027, Δ^2 = .013). Female candidates (M = 2.09) were perceived as being less likely than male candidates (M = 1.87) to beat incumbents.

The second research question pertains to the potential impact of subjects' attitude toward equal opportunity on their assessments of the non-White fictional candidates. As shown in Table 7.1, this attitude significantly influences the subjects' *support* for non-White candidates (t = –3.86, p < .001, R square change = .064) when other demographic, interaction, and exposure variables are held constant. However, when assessing the non-White candidate's *electability* for a Pennsylvanian congressional seat, the experiment participants were not affected by their belief in equality (t = .76, p = .45, R square change = .003). These two results are quite interesting because the former seems to indicate a subjective or idealistic voting inclination, whereas the latter unveils a more objective or realistic evaluation.

The first research hypothesis was intended to examine the potential gap between a participant's own voting likelihood and his or her assessment of others' voting for non-White candidates. Two dependent variables were used in the hypothesis testing: (a) the likelihood the participant would vote for the candidate, and (b) the extent to which the candidate reflects the participant's view. Two pairs of t tests were executed. The results show that both differences of likelihood are

Table 7.1
Predicting *Voting* for Non-White Candidates

Block	Beta	t	p	ΔR²
1 Interaction with the candidate's race	−0.09	−1.39	0.17	
Media use	0.01	0.21	0.83	0.009
2 Male	0.02	0.24	0.81	
White	−0.09	−1.24	0.22	
Age	−0.18	−2.49	0.01	0.073
Education level	−0.09	−1.22	0.22	
Income level	−0.03	−0.37	0.71	
3 Index of equality attitude	−0.27	−3.86	0.00	0.064
(Constant)		9.98	0.00	

$F = 4.237$, df = 8,197, $p < .001$. $\qquad\qquad$ $R^2 = 0.147$

statistically significant. Participants see themselves as more likely than others to support non-White candidates (self $M = 1.79$ vs. others $M = 2.05$, $t = -5.141$, df = 221, $p < .001$), and they see the non-White candidates reflecting their views more than others' views (self $M = 1.77$ vs. others $M = 2.00$, $t = -4.699$, df = 220, $p < .001$). This finding shows a more pessimistic assessment of others' view on non-White candidates. Thus, the first hypothesis is supported.

Our second hypothesis focuses on the potential influence of one's formal and informal interaction with the race of the candidate. Similar to the procedure of the prior tests, only those subjects who were exposed to the stimuli of non-White candidates were included in the regression models. Also, because vicarious exposure to non-White groups through the media could elevate one's familiarity, media exposure variable—including exposure to newspaper, TV news, and Web news—was incorporated into the regression model. The results (see Tables 7.1 and 7.2) show that the interaction predictor in both regression models (voting and electability) is not statistically significant. However, according to the beta values of the two independent variables, it appears that an individual's experience of interaction with the race of the feature candidate plays a slightly greater role in predicting his voting tendency than his assessment of the non-White candidate's electability. Even with the share of media exposure variable included, the entire block in both cases contributes less than 1% of the total variance to the regression models. Therefore, the second hypothesis is rejected.

Table 7.2
Predicting *Electability* of Non-White Candidates

Block	Beta	t	p	ΔR^2
1 Interaction with the candidate's race	−0.01	−0.10	0.92	
Media use	−0.06	−0.88	0.38	0.009
2 Male	0.15	2.18	0.03	
White	0.01	0.09	0.93	
Age	−0.17	−2.36	0.02	0.065
Education level	0.09	1.26	0.21	
Income level	−0.05	−0.61	0.54	
3 Index of equality attitude	0.06	0.76	0.45	0.003
(Constant)		5.78	0.00	

$F = 2.063$, df = 8,197, $p < .041$. $\qquad$ $R^2 = 0.077$

A couple of other findings in the regression tables are worth men-tioning. Overall, demographics contribute to the dependent variables (voting and electability) substantially. Among them, in particular, age is negatively related to being willing to support non-White candidates (beta = −.018, $t = -2.49$, $p = .01$) and also is negatively related to posi-tive assessments of non-White candidates (beta = −.017, $t = -2.36$, $p = .02$). This finding is rather intriguing. Another interesting demographic determinant is gender. Albeit with statistical insignificance ($p = .81$), males are less likely than females to support non-White candidates, and men are prone to see a slim chance for non-White candidates to win public offices ($p = .03$).

CONCLUSION AND DISCUSSION

This study set out to examine the impact of race and gender on political judgment and led to some intriguing results. For one thing, race turns out to be a greater factor than gender in predicting people's perception of a candidate's electability. In particular, African- and Asian American candidates appear to be in a disadvantaged position because the electorate simply cannot picture them as winning seats in the Congress. Without the "winning picture" in voters' heads, it would be extremely hard for them to show any type of support to these two groups of candidates. The com-mon scenario that African- and Asian American candidates would face is exactly like the scenario faced by Howard Dean in the campaign of 2004: Without the prospect of winning, few votes are cast for him. Therefore, the fulfilling prophecy of the public could deeply hurt the participation and representation of these two racial groups in the political arena.

This study generates some good news for female political candidates. It appears that people look at them as serious contenders for political office and perceive them to be *almost* as electable as men. Although in reality women are still outnumbered by men in the Congress and other levels of public offices, this research finding may shed new light on the prospect of women attaining public offices at the federal level. The public in general seems accustomed to seeing female politicians. Perhaps the political system can invest more energy and time to recruit and retain women as viable candidates; however, more motivated women politicians are needed to balance the gender gap in American politics.

It is surprising that the interracial interaction variable fails to predict one's likelihood of voting for non-White candidates. The vicarious interaction—media exposure—also does not affect people's voting and winning assessments. In essence, what this finding suggests is that one's familiarity or understanding of a race does not equate his support for candidates of that race. In other words, a person's political judgment and evaluation are not based on one's personal experience with the race of the candidate, but something potentially more complicated and tactical. This finding, however, could be positive for non-White candidates especially if they run campaigns in regions where the population of their race is small.

The most significant single determinant of the regression models from this study is a person's belief in equality. It systematically predicts well for one's own support for non-White candidates, but not so well for assessments of others' political action. This finding makes sense because believing in equality does not block one's capability to objectively assess political situations. The problem, however, is how far one can go—ideally—in the face of the cruel political reality. If the assessments are overwhelmingly negative for a person's favored non-White candidate, will she be able to stick it out to the end or go the extra mile to support her candidate? Will she not cave in to peer pressure or strategic voting? These questions lead us to the impact of third-person effect on voting.

The findings show that, overall, participants demonstrated a gap between their voting likelihood and others' for non-White candidates. It is highly possible that this gap is a pure miscalculation of their—and perhaps others'—voting intentions. But if the majority of voters had this tendency to overestimate other people's biases and reservations, then their situation analysis would be almost always unfavorable to non-White candidates. Additionally, given that many voters have access to polling results and ponder about the electability factor before even considering supporting or casting their votes, it will always prove a daunting task for African- and Asian American candidates to campaign and win elections.

Unfortunately, this study does not deliver a rosy picture for those aspiring minority candidates nor a prospect of truly diverse political representation in the near future. However, it is important to bear in mind that our conclusions are derived from an experiment with unknown, fictional candidates in an election race unattached to the participants. As they are in every race, the contexts and situations of real elections vary dramatically and could very well affect election outcomes. Sometimes a candidate's charisma or popularity can simply overcome the race or gender barrier. There are bound to be other crucial factors that determine the result in real races. This is exactly one of the shortcomings in experiment research. Future studies should benefit from data of real elections when people can form more grounded opinions about real candidates of different races and gender. The findings of this study should only serve as a springboard for better understanding the impact of race and gender on electability.

REFERENCES

Affigne, T. (2000). Latino politics in the United States: An introduction. *PS, Political Science & Politics, 33*(3), 523–527.

Allport, G. W. (1954). *The nature of prejudice.* Reading, MA: Addison-Wesley.

Amir, Y. (1969). Contact hypothesis in ethnic relations. *Psychological Bulletin, 71*(5), 319–342.

Anti-Defamation League. (2001, April 25). *American attitudes toward Chinese and Asian Americans.* http://www.adl.org/misc/american_attitudes_towards_chinese.asp.

Armstrong, B. G., Neuendorf, K. A., & Brentar, J. E. (1992). TV entertainment, news, and racial perceptions of college students. *Journal of Communication, 42*(3), 153–176.

Barnett, J. (2001, May 26). Wu accesses federal office of racial bias. The *Oregonian*, p. A01.

Bernstein, A. (2004, June 14). Women's pay: Why the gap remains a chasm; A new study spells out the costly impact of family obligations. *Business Week*, p. 58.

Bertrand, M., & Hallock, K. F. (2001). The gender gap in top corporate jobs. *Industrial and Labor Relations Review, 55*(1), 3–21.

Bertrand, M., & Mullainathan, S. (2004). Are Emily and Greg more employable than Lakisha and Jamal? A field experiment on labor market discrimination. *The American Economic Review, 94*(4), 991–1011.

Blumler, J. G., & Katz, E. (Eds.). (1974). *The uses of mass communications: Current perspectives on gratifications research*. Beverly Hills, CA: Sage.

Brooks, D. (2004, January 31). Electing the electable. *New York Times*, Sec. A, p. 17.

Busselle, R., & Crandall, H. (2002). Television viewing and perceptions about race differences in socioeconomic success. *Journal of Broadcasting & Electronic Media, 46*(2), 265–282.

Calmes, J. (2007, January 11). Democrats' litmus: Electability, key issue for 2008 race poses hurdles for Clinton, Obama. *Wall Street Journal*, p. A6.

Cortese, A. C. (2004). *Provocateur: Images of women and minorities in advertising*. New York: Rowman & Littlefield.

Davidson, W. P. (1983). The third-person effect in communication. *Public Opinion Quarterly, 47*, 1–13.

Dixon, T. L., & Linz, D. (2000). Overrepresentation and underrepresentation of African Americans and Latinos as law breakers on television news. *Journal of Communication, 50*(2), 131–154.

Dovidio, J. F., Gaertner, S. L., Nier, J. A., Kawakami, K., & Hodson, G. (2004). Contemporary racial bias: When good people do bad things. In A. G. Miller (Ed.), *The social psychology of good and evil* (pp. 141–167). New York: Guilford.

Entman, R. M. (1990). Modern racism and images of Blacks in local television news. *Critical Studies in Mass Communication, 7*, 332–346.

Entman, R. M. (1994). Blacks in television news: Television, modern racism and cultural changes. *Journalism Quarterly, 69*(2), 341–361.

Entman, R., & Rojecki, A. (2000). *The Black image in the White mind*. Chicago, IL: University of Chicago Press.

Fujioka, Y. (1999). Television portrayals and African-American stereotypes: Examination of television effects when direct contact is lacking. *Journalism and Mass Communication Quarterly, 76*(1), 52–75.

Gandy, O., Jr., & Baron, J. (1992). Inequality: It's all in the way you look at it. *Communication Research, 25*(5), 505–527.

Gerbner, G., Gross, L., Jackson-Beeck, M., Jeffries-Fox, S., & Signorielli, N. (1978). Television violence profile no. 9. *Journal of Communication, 28*(3), 176–207.

Gerbner, G., Gross, L., Morgan, M., & Signorielli, N. (1980). The "mainstreaming" of America: Violence profile no. 11. *Journal of Communication, 30*(3), 10–29.

Gerbner, G., Gross, L., Signorielli, N., Morgan, M., & Jackson-Beeck, M. (1979). The demonstration of power: Violence profile no. 10. *Journal of Communication, 29*(3), 177–196.

Gilliam, F. D., & Iyengar, S. (1998, August). *The corrosive influence of local television news on racial beliefs*. Paper resented to the annual meeting of the Association for Education in Journalism and Mass Communication, Baltimore, MD.

Goffman, E. (1976). *Gender advertisement*. New York: Harper & Row.

Gordon, M. E., Slade, L. A., & Schmitt, N. (1986). The "science of the sophomore" revisited: From conjecture to empiricism. *Academy of Management Review, 11*(1), 191–207.

Hamamoto, D. Y. (1994). *Monitored peril: Asian Americans and the politics of TV representation*. Minneapolis: University of Minnesota Press.

He's got a ticket to ride. (2004, February 24). The *Economist, 370*(8362), 27–30.

Ho, C., & Jackson, J. W. (2001). Attitudes toward Asian Americans: Theory and measurement. *Journal of Applied Social Psychology, 31*(8), 1553–1581.

Kilbourne, J. (1999). *Deadly persuasion: Why women and girls must fight the addictive power of advertising*. New York: The Free Press.

Larson, S. G. (2006). *Media & minorities: The politics of race in news and entertainment*. Lanham, MD: Rowman & Littlefield.

Lee, J. (1994). A look at Asians as portrayed in the news. *Editor & Publisher, 127*(18), 56.

Lee, R. G. (1999). *Orientals: Asian Americans in popular culture*. Philadelphia, PA: Temple University Press.

Lee, T., & Hwang, F. H. (2002). Portrayal of women in movie ads changes little from 1963–1993. *Newspaper Research Journal, 23*(4), 86–90.

Lester, P. M. (Ed.). (1996). *Images that injure: Pictorial stereotypes in the media*. Westport, CT: Praeger.

Meyers, M. (Ed.). (1999). *Mediated women: Representations in popular culture*. Cresskill, NJ: Hampton Press.

Meyrowitz, J. (1992, March/April). The press rejects a candidate. *Columbia Journalism Review*, pp. 46–48.

Peffley, M., & Hurwitz, J. (1998). Whites' stereotypes of Blacks: Sources and political consequences. In J. Hurwitz & M. Peffley (Eds.), *Perception and prejudice: Race and politics in the United States* (pp. 58–99). New Haven, CT: Yale University Press.

Perloff, R. M. (1993). Third-perfect effect research 1983–1992: A review and synthesis. *International Journal of Public Opinion Research, 5*, 167–184.

Perloff, R. M. (1999). The third-person effect: A critical review and synthesis. *Media Psychology, 1*, 353–378.

Pettigrew T. F. (1998). Applying social psychology to international social issues. *Journal of Social Issues, 54*(4), 663–675.

Rada, J. A. (2000). A new piece of the puzzle: Examining effects of television portrayals of African Americans. *Journal of Broadcasting & Electronic Media, 44*(4), 704–715.

Rubin, A. M., & Perse, E. M. (1987). Audience activity and television news gratifications. *Communication Research, 14*, 58–84.

Schuman, H., Steeh, C., Bobo, L., & Krysan, M. (1997). *Racial attitudes in America: Trends and interpretations*. Cambridge, MA: Harvard University Press.

Severin, W. J., & Tankard, J. W., Jr. (1997). *Communication theories: Origins, methods, and uses in the mass media*. New York: Longman.

Shaw, D. (2004, February 1). Media matters; Pundits' prophesies may transform voters' reality. *Los Angeles Times*, p. F20.

Signorielli, N., & Morgan, M. (Eds.). (1990). *Cultivation analysis: New directions in media effects research*. Newbury Park, CA: Sage.

Slater, M. D. (2003). Alienation, aggression, and sensation seeking as predictors of adolescent use of violent film, computer, and website content. *Journal of Communication, 53*(1), 105–121.

Sniderman, P. M., Brody, R. A., & Tetlock, P. E. (1991). *Reasoning and choice: Explorations in political psychology.* Cambridge, MA: Harvard University Press.

Sniderman, P. M., & Carmines, E. G. (1997). *Reaching beyond race.* Cambridge, MA: Harvard University Press.

Sniderman, P. M., Piazza, T., Tetlock, P. E., & Kendrick, A. (1991). The new racism. *American Journal of Political Science, 35*(2), 423–447.

Tan, A., Fujioka, Y., & Lucht, N. (1997). Native American stereotypes, TV portrayals, and personal contact. *Journalism and Mass Communication Quarterly, 74,* 265–284.

Tuch, S. A., & Martin, J. K. (Eds.). (1997). *Racial attitudes in the 1990s: Continuity and change.* Westport, CT: Praeger.

Tung, W. (1974). *The Chinese in America.* Dobbs Ferry, NY: Oceana Publications.

U.S. Census Bureau. (2005, September 8). *Hispanic heritage month 2005: September 15–Oct. 15.* Retrieved from http://www.census.gov/Press-Release/www/releases/archives/facts_for_features_special_editions/005338.html

Valentino, N. A. (1999). Crime news and the priming of racial attitudes during evaluations of the president. *Public Opinion Quarterly, 63*(3), 293–320.

Welch, S., & Studlar, D. T. (1996). The opportunity structure for women's candidates and electability in Britain and the United States. *Political Research Quarterly, 49*(4), 861–874.

Wu, F. H. (2002). *Yellow: Race in America beyond black and white.* New York: Basic Books.

Wu, J. Y. S., & Song, M. (2000). *Asian American studies: A reader.* New Brunswick, NJ: Rutgers University Press.

Yee, A. H. (1992). Asians as stereotypes and students: Misperceptions that persist. *Educational Psychology Review, 4*(1), 95–133.

Chapter 8

Closing Thoughts and Recommendations

CLOSING THOUGHTS AND PREDICTIONS

We believe previous chapters have provided a rather comprehensive picture of issues regarding Asian Americans in the context of the news media and politics. In this chapter, we summarize our thoughts and offer a few recommendations.

Mainly due to our quantitative training, in previous chapters we devoted more of our attention to data interpretations instead of the implications of findings. This chapter is our opportunity to share our comments without feeling obligated to add a footnote or reference to everything we say.

In general, the news media, at least newspapers, try to provide a rather quantitatively balanced coverage between Asian American candidates and their opponents. However, when we dug deeper, we found that news reports have consistently, although not frequently, reflected a mentality that considers Asian Americans politicians as aliens and outsiders. Their Euro-American opponents, however, have not received similar portrayal. Based on this finding, we argue that if Asian American *elites* running for major public offices are not considered "authentic" Americans, everyday Asian Americans would likely receive the same or worse treatment by their fellow Americans. This extrapolation is beyond our scope of inquiry, but it is definitely worth pondering.

As mentioned in our introduction, the recent anti-immigrant trend in the United States has become stronger, which certainly does not work to the advantage of Asian Americans. Furthermore, the Virginia Tech incident in April 2007, in which Seung-Hui Cho killed more than 30 people, might have negatively affected the overall image of all Asian immigrants, not just Korean Americans. Nevertheless, a few findings across various chapters suggest that there is some hope for Asian Americans who are interested in entering politics and pursuing public offices. For example, public attitudes toward this racial group as a whole have been improving in recent years. Younger voters are more willing to vote for Asian American candidates. Also, citizens who believe in equality are more likely to support Asian American candidates. In addition, female Asian American candidates are not necessarily at a disadvantage in comparison with their male counterparts. Therefore, we believe there is an increasingly friendlier environment for Asian Americans to run for public offices.

RECOMMENDATIONS FOR ASIAN AMERICAN PUBLIC OFFICE SEEKERS

We have the following recommendations for the next generation of Asian American public office seekers. First, run in geographic areas that have a significant population of racial minorities—especially Asian Americans—as well as young voters. Second, keep in mind that your own and other ethnic groups within the Asian American community may not automatically support you. Third, you are more likely to win in areas that are considered more liberal, where the principle of equality is valued and the electorate is more open minded. For example, the number of women, gays, and lesbians who hold public offices would be a good indicator of that type of region. Fourth, your opponents and the news media are likely to draw attention to your perceived foreignness. When they consciously or unconsciously disclose their racial bias, be prepared to take strategic steps to remind voters—and your "accusers"—that you are as American as your opponents.

Earlier in the book, we argued that many Americans simply do not see Asian Americans as mayors, governors, senators, and so on. The best way to counter this perception is reality. Personally, we can relate to this situation. Although we have been full-time faculty for more than 10 years, many people we have encountered, including a few of our own students, still think we are graduate students or teaching assistants before entering our classes. There is nothing wrong with being either, but we have moved beyond that station in life.

Although we would prefer to attribute this misperception to our youthful appearance, we know the real reason: Asian American professors are a rarity in higher education, especially in journalism mass communication and schools. We are grateful that the pioneers studied in this book have paved the way for aspiring Asian American public servants. Regardless of the outcome, Woo, Locke, Wu, Fong, Jindal—and others we have not studied—have made a critical contribution by participating in elections as candidates. We hope more Asian Americans will run for public office at different levels. Once our fellow Americans are used to seeing Asian Americans running and winning, the idea of Asian Americans as elected officials may no longer seem foreign (pun intended). More important, once you win, we hope you will be an excellent leader and public servant; otherwise you will add to the negative stereotype that Asian Americans cannot be trusted.

RECOMMENDATIONS FOR THE NEWS MEDIA

We have two suggestions for news organizations. Many of you have hired or assigned seasoned or special reporters to cover issues related to racial/ethnic minorities, and we thank you for that. Having one or two in your organization, however, is not enough. We urge you to hire more members of various racial or ethnic backgrounds because they will enrich your newsrooms and improve the quality of reporting in general. Good journalism, we believe, is good for business.

Second, an increasing number of news outlets have implemented a policy not to identify criminal suspects' racial backgrounds, at least in words. (We understand that showing photographs or video footage is different.) We think it is a good practice, and we encourage all news organizations to consider similar policies when their staff reporters cover racial minorities in general. Although we strongly believe in celebrating diversity, there are times, we believe, the media should focus on similarities rather than differences.

We also have a few recommendations for journalists when facing Asian Americans or any other minorities in the stories they work on. There are a variety of means to advance journalistic quality—awareness and sensitivity could be the first phase. The traditional journalistic tenets, such as impartiality, fairness, and objectivity, help, too. When you cover a political candidate who happens to be a member of a racial or ethnic minority, we urge you to ask yourself three questions. First, do you have a good reason to mention his or her racial or ethnic background in each report? We believe that there are occasions in which you should, but most of the time that should not be necessary. Second, if you feel the need to address one candidate's racial/ethnic/family heritage for any reason, try to do so for his or her opponents, too. If you identify someone as fourth-generation Japanese American, for instance, shouldn't you mention that his or her opponent is seventh-generation German American? Third, carefully examine your questions for all candidates by asking yourself whether such questions reflect the ideology of treating a particular candidate as a foreigner or any other characters. A good example of such a question is that, if China (or another country) and the United States were at war, which side would you support? Unless a candidate is Native American (or Hawaiian), his or her ancestors all came from somewhere outside of the United States. Questions that are not logical or legitimate should be avoided at all times.

THE BIG "WHY" AND A BRIGHTER FUTURE

Throughout the book, you probably have been wondering why Asian Americans are perceived as perpetual foreigners or why racism in general exists. Many scholars cited in this book have provided helpful insights, such as historical roots, power imbalance, and an ingroup versus outgroup mentality. We believe that one's unique culture should be cherished and celebrated, but if or when differences might lead to unfair treatment, a closer examination is needed, which is one of the reasons why this book was written. In approaching the end of our book, let us share our speculation about the "why."

Throughout human history, and still in today's culture, the ideology of separation and division is promoted, reinforced, or at least taken for granted. For example, we see movies and books featuring hostile space aliens and foreigners, in which war heroes who have killed a large number of enemies are glorified and worshiped. Rivalries between schools and professional sports teams (and particularly their fans) are fanatic in many parts of the country as well as the world. The Red State–Blue State divide seems even more pronounced in recent U.S. elections. Gays and lesbians cannot legally marry in most states and nations. Women cannot hold the same clergy positions as their male counterparts in many religions. People use many excuses for hostilities and discriminations, but we argue that the real issue is unity versus separation.

Of course there are differences among people, but many have forgotten—and have been encouraged to forget—that "we are one" in essence and, therefore, should be treated equally. Recent biological discoveries can prove how similar humans of different races are. Differential or discriminatory treatment of certain groups of people is a natural consequence of this forgotten fact. If we agree that the mentality of division is a problem, or *the* problem, then we know how to overcome it. We need to learn to see others as one with us, and the mass media, we believe, should lead the way.

Only time will tell whether candidates of Asian ancestry for public offices—and Asian Americans in general—will eventually be considered and treated as part of the mainstream in America. We are optimistic because we have seen the latest presidential election cycle in which Hillary Clinton and Barack Obama competed in the Democratic Party contest; and the Republican Party nominated Sarah Palin as its vice-presidential candidate. The result of the 2008 election made history. Now in the Obama Administration, Gary Locke—who is featured in this book—is the Secretary of Commerce. His fellow Asian American, Steven Chu, heads the Department of Energy. Perhaps this country's political landscape is poised for great, positive changes. We shall remain hopeful in the process.

Author Index

Subject Index

Printed in the United States
145033LV00005B/3/P